The
Mature Woman
in America

A Selected Annotated Bibliography
1979-1982

NATIONAL COUNCIL ON THE AGING, INC.

The National Council on the Aging, Inc.
600 Maryland Avenue, S.W., West Wing 100
Washington, D.C. 20024

     The National Council on the Aging, Inc., established
in 1950, is the national organization for professionals and
volunteers who work to improve the quality of life for older
Americans. Headquartered in Washington, D.C., within view
of the U.S. Capitol, NCOA is a nonprofit central, national
resource for research, planning, training, information
dissemination, technical assistance, advocacy, program and
standards development and publications that relate to all
aspects of aging.
     Noted for addressing, with a strong voice, the issues
that profoundly affect older citizens, NCOA, for more than
three decades, has played a major role in awakening the
nation to both the needs and potential of its older citizens.

President
Arthur S. Flemming, J.D., Washington, D.C.
   Director, National Coalition
   for Quality Integrated Education

Vice Presidents
Anna V. Brown, Cleveland, Ohio
   Director, Department of Aging

James T. Sykes, Madison, Wisconsin
   Director of Public Service
   The Wisconsin Cheeseman

Secretary
Edith Sherman, Ph.D., Denver, Colorado
   Retired Director, Institute of Gerontology
   University of Denver

Assistant Secretary
Barbara Sklar, San Francisco, California
   Director, Geriatric Services
   Mount Zion Hospital and Medical Center

Treasurer
James H. Agee, Washington, D.C.
   Vice President, First American Bank, N.A.

Assistant Treasurer
Roger A. Baird, Menasha, Wisconsin
   Attorney, retired Secretary, Kimberly-Clark

Executive Director
Jack Ossofsky

THE MATURE WOMAN IN AMERICA

A SELECTED ANNOTATED BIBLIOGRAPHY

1979-1982

COMPILED BY

ELEANOR F. DOLAN AND DOROTHY M. GROPP

THE NATIONAL COUNCIL ON THE AGING, INC.
1984

Compilers' note:

Eleanor F. Dolan, Specialist for Graduate Academic Education of the Office
of Education (retired) and more recently Executive Secretary of the National
Council of Administrative Women in Education.

Dorothy M. Gropp, Associate Librarian, The National Council on the Aging, Inc.

Library of Congress Cataloging in Publication Data

    Dolan, Eleanor F. (Eleanor Frances), 1907-
      The mature woman in America.

      1. Aged women--United States--Bibliography.
    2. Middle aged women--United States--Bibliography.
    3. Library of the National Council on the Aging.
    I. Gropp, Dorothy M., 1907-   . II. Title.
    Z7164.04D64 1984 [HQ1064.U5] 016.3054   84-3292
    ISBN 0-910883-02-5

CONTENTS

FOREWORD

This selected annotated bibliography of over 420 items, on the mature woman in America and the policies which affect her, covers the period from 1979 through 1982, with a few earlier and later imprints. The materials stress statistics and research, both of which reflect current greatly increased interest in women and their roles in modern America.

The annotations have been prepared mostly by Eleanor F. Dolan and Dorothy M. Gropp, with contributions by John B. Balkema, formerly of the Library staff at the National Council on the Aging. Mrs. Gropp, associate librarian, has acted as editorial associate. The work could not have been completed without the constant, professional and creative work of Mrs. Gropp. This manuscript preparation is gratefully acknowledged to be the work of Suzanne Levesque, also of the Library. The careful proofreading and helpful editing of Nellie Apanasewicz have also contributed to the acccuracy of the finished product. Errors of fact or interpretation are the responsibility of the compilers.

All the literature cited in this bibliography is to be found in the Library of the National Council on the Aging.

Eleanor F. Dolan

INTRODUCTION

Gerontologists increasingly are observing that aging in America, as well as in a number of other societies, is largely a woman's issue. While many characteristics and problems of older women are common to older people of both sexes, several salient phenomena have impressed upon gerontolgists and policy makers the need to devote greater attention to the circumstances of older women.

For instance, the proportion of older women to men, 65 years and older, today is approximately 1.5 to 1, and for individuals 75 years and older the ratio dramatically increases to 1.9 woman for every male. By the turn of the century it is projected that there will be some 19.1 million women over 65 and 12.7 men over 65. Because the life expectancy for women is greater than for men, older women are much more likely than men to live alone; in 1980 half of the women 65-74 were widowed, divorced or never married, and 70% of women aged 75+ were widows.

Until the past decade or so, older women remained a hidden or largely ignored majority of America's older population. The recent growth in literature on the older woman reflects the ever growing attention which her circumstances have attracted. Just in terms of the citations included in this bibliography, we see that 59 entries are listed for 1979, 79 for 1980, 92 for 1981, and 145 for 1982.

Demgraphics alone do not explain today's increased interest in the older woman. Rather, changing social attitudes account for this significant development which is reflected in the continually increasing outpouring of literature and concern. The gradual emergence of women of all ages into the labor market during and since World War II, with their collateral participation in many other activities outside the home, has brought them more and more to public and scholarly notice.

The older or mature woman has entered this stream of women flowing from the shelter of the home into the bustle of the competitive world for several reasons. The changing marital scene leaves many midlife women unmarried, divorced, or widows in poor economic circumstances; consequently, they are faced with earning their entire living, or at least augmenting an inadequate retirement income. Furthermore, private pensions and Social Security alike have been geared in the past to the concept of the husband as breadwinner for a wife and children and have been unresponsive to the circumstances of the widow-survivor.

No precise and widely acceptable definition of "older" women exists, due to the variable determinants used by scholars, researchers, the government, and the general public in establishing who is an older woman. For purposes of drawing Social Security benefits, a woman must be 62 years of age, yet the U.S. Department of Labor considers women over the age of 40 to be "older" persons. This "moveable" age suggests that there are interrelated and continuous events associated with aging (for both men and women) that span the several decades before and after that watershed age of 65, so popularly considered to denote the onset of old age.

While most of the entries in this bibliography relate to women in their later decades, other entries, for example, concern the problems of women re-entering the workforce in their 40's, 50's, and even 60's. Given the life expectancy of the woman aged 65 today (of living past age 83), this bibliography has adopted the term "mature" woman as representing the concept that the recognizable aging process for a woman begins in her mid 40's.

Several bibliographies published in the mid-1970s on the subject of older women are useful contributions to the field. Notable among these reference works are: EMERGING ROLE OF MATURE WOMEN, by Anna Elkin (Federation of Employment and Guidance Service, New York, 1976. 20 pp.); THE OLDER WOMEN IN PRINT AND FILM, by Carol Hollenshead (Institute of Gerontology, University of Michigan, Ann Arbor, 1977. 52 pp.); and, AGE IS BECOMING: AN ANNOTATED BIBLIOGRAPHY ON WOMEN AND AGING, by Interface Bibliographers (Glide Publications, San Francisco, 1976. 36 pp.).

More recently, Dr. Audrey Borenstein has performed a valuable service with her historical treatment, OLDER WOMEN IN TWENTIETH CENTURY AMERICA: A SELECTED ANNOTATED BIBLIOGRAPHY (Garland Publishing, Inc., New York, 1982. 364 pp.). Aside from materials in social gerontology, this work is particularly rich in references to autobiographies, oral histories, novels, short stories, personal documents, and journals, all of which fall outside the intended scope of THE MATURE WOMAN IN AMERICA bibliography. While the two bibliographies seem to overlap, the Borenstein work includes comparatively fewer citations to non-literary works with an imprint date after 1978. This comment is meant to suggest that these two bibliographies supplement each other, and the researcher would do well to use the two in tandem to cover the literature up through 1982, and into early 1983.

THE MATURE WOMAN IN AMERICA bibliography contains 423 citations to literature specifically treating the older woman. Five citations are to imprints prior to 1979 which were included because of their "classical" importance, and 43 are to monographs and journal articles which appeared in early 1983. Annotations for each citation attempt not only to summarize the salient points of that selection, but also to mention whether it contains statistical information.

Compilation of THE MATURE WOMAN IN AMERICA bibliography began in fall 1982 as a response to the growing number of inquiries the NCOA Library was receiving on older women's issues. Initially, the bibliography proposed to be an "in-house" resource of current materials in the NCOA Library for two groups: the NCOA staff in their widening interest in the status of women, and visiting researchers and readers to the NCOA Library pursuing similar interests. As work on the bibliography progressed and the great extent of relevant materials on the subject found in the Library became evident, a decision was made to expand the coverage to 1979-1982 imprints, and to prepare the work for distribution to the general public in a commercial form. The bibliographers adhered to the original decision to cite only materials in the NCOA Library, however. To have attempted a definitive bibliography by searching out non-NCOA materials would have meant delay in publishing at the expense of a not greatly augmented bibliography.

To compile THE MATURE WOMAN IN AMERICA bibliography, a thorough search was made of materials under pertinent subject headings in the Library's card catalog as was a systematic review of the shelf list of the book and vertical file matierals under appropriate classification areas. In addition, a careful examination of all books in the general gerontology collection was made to find chapters and sections relating to the mature woman. Each piece of literature was individually reviewed in the preparation of the annotation. To complete the bibliography in the area of journal articles, a careful review was made of the literature abstracted in CURRENT LITERATURE ON AGING (NCOA's quarterly abstracting service in this subject field).

The bibliography incorporates the following types of literature: books, pamphlets, bibliographies, directories, guides, journal articles, conference reports, statistical reports, government documents (especially those from Congressional committees on aging), and some unpublished papers and reports. Each entry in the bibliography, listed in alphabetical order by author, includes: author, title, publisher, imprint date, and paging.

To facilitate the use of the bibliography, a full subject index has been appended. As many monographs and journal articles treat more than a single subject, the index lists such materials under multiple subject heads. In this way, the minor or secondary aspect of the work is brought to the attention of the user in addition to the main or primary aspect. Thus for example, a study of the employment patterns of displaced homemakers will be found under "Employment," "Displaced Homemakers," and "Re-Entry to Work Force."

Main entries in the subject index include among others: Bibliography (51 items); Blacks (27); Caregivers (11); Divorce (12); Employment (60); Family Life (22); History (13); Income (28); Life Style (15); Marital Status (16); Middle Age (16); Organizations and Networks (14); Public/ Social Policy (46); Re-Entry to work Force (15); Retirement (24); Retirement Adjustment (19); Sex Comparisons/Differences (40); Social Role (13); Social Security (37); Statistics (77); Stress and Crises (14); and Widows (38). Other entries with one to several items include: Alcoholism; Battered Women; Childlessness; Church Attendance; Cosmetics; Daydreams; Group Psychotherapy; Health Clubs; Obesity; Pioneers; Respite Care; Single Room Occupancy; Suburban Women; Time; Women in Advertisements.

In the subject index, the reference is to the author, by his/her last name and initials. If this author has written more than one item included in this bibliography, his/her name is followed by the first word or words of each title, for exact identification in the main bibliography.

All materials cited in this bibliography are available in the NCOA Library. Monographs may be borrowed through an inter-library loan request and journal literature may be consulted in the library. The NCOA Library comprises some 14,500 books, principally in socio-economic gerontology, with 30 drawers of vertical file materials, all completely processed in the card catalog. The Library collection and its services are available to the public for on-premises use.

THE MATURE WOMAN IN AMERICA

AGING AWARENESS: AN ANNOTATED BIBLIOGRAPHY. 2d ed. Pittsburgh,
    Pennsylvania, Generations Together, 1982. 83 pp.

    A bibliography compiled to encourage better understanding by the
    young of the elderly, and better recognition of the resources of the
    elderly. Few titles single out the elderly woman until the last sec-
    tion, "Elderly in Children's Books," where 57 such female oriented
    titles are given, mostly about grandmothers. The books in this
    section are graded from pre-school through grade 8.

Allyn, Mildred V., comp. ABOUT AGING: A CATALOG OF FILMS, WITH A SPECIAL
    SECTION ON VIDEOCASSETTES. 4th ed. Los Angeles, Ethel Percy Andrus
    Gerontology Center, University of Southern California, 1979. 249 pp.

    This 4th edition follows the format of previous editions: an alpha-
    betical listing of titles of 16mm films, videocassettes, and feature
    length films. Information on the titles in each category includes
    annotation, running time of the film, producer, cost (sale or rent),
    and where to procure it. In the subject index under "Women," this
    4th edition lists 58 titles. The 1981 "Supplement to the Fourth
    Edition" lists another 29 titles.

Almvig, Chris. INVISIBLE MINORITY: AGING AND LESBIANISM. Utica, New York,
    Utica College of Syracuse University, December 1982. 198 pp.

    Report based on a questionnaire, "Aging and Lesbian/Gay Male"
    sent to 74 lesbians and 236 gay men over 50. Questionnaire (pp. 175-
    179) had 44 questions with detailed sub-questions. The results of
    the survey are summarized in Ch. 4, with tables accompanying the
    summary statements, which deal with the common experience, feelings,
    demography, relationships, and history of the lesbian of today.
    Resources, pp. 196-198, lists organizations offering assistance to
    lesbians and gay men.

Alston, Letitia T. and Jon P. Alston. Religion and the Older Woman. In:
    Fuller, Marie M. and Cora Ann Martin, eds. OLDER WOMEN: LAVENDER
    ROSE GRAY PANTHER. Springfield, Illinois, Charles C. Thomas,
    Publisher, 1980. pp. 262-278.

    This paper is concerned with the question of whether or not life-
    cycle stages influence religious behavior, and focuses on selected
    status and age variables that may be associated with frequency of
    church attendance among women over fifty years of age. The author
    draws two conclusions: today's older woman is far more likely to be
    a frequent church attender than her male counterpart or today's
    younger woman; and the effects of variables (marital status,
    children, and work status) are less than were expected. Age is a
    more important variable for predicting church attendance than a
    woman's involvement in other activity roles.

American Council of Life Insurance. OLDER AMERICANS. Washington, D.C.,
     1982. 32 pp.

     Insurance companies are aware of the increasing proportion of the
     65+ age population and have become aware also that there are to be
     increasingly more women than men in this same age bracket.
     Companies, therefore, are alert to adjust their policies to the
     changing conditions. This pamphlet presents research background for
     changes, discussing not only the number of older women but also their
     conditions. There are 23 tables, many of them by sex.

Andre, Rae. HOMEMAKERS: THE FORGOTTEN WORKERS. Chicago, University of
     Chicago Press, 1981. 299 pp.

     Examines the lives and problems of American women whose main occupa-
     tion is homemaker, noting that the problems of the older unemployed
     homemaker are particularly acute, and suggesting how the problems
     might be solved. Ch. 10, "Change in the House--and in the Senate"
     (pp. 207-228), discusses proposed changes in most of the areas in
     which women encounter discrimination or nonconsideration.

Antonucci, Toni C. Longitudinal and Cross-Sectional Data Sources on Women
     in the Middle Years. In: Giele, Janet Zollinger, ed. WOMEN IN THE
     MIDDLE YEARS: CURRENT KNOWLEDGE AND DIRECTIONS FOR RESEARCH AND
     POLICY. New York, John Wiley & Sons, 1982. pp. 241-274.

     Some of the data to support the thesis that both men and women con-
     tinue to grow and develop over their entire life course are already
     available. This chapter is designed to present some idea of these
     resources and help answer questions about work- and personality-
     related issues of middle-aged women. Five types of data sets are
     shown: large data sets; fertility-related studies; longitudinal data
     sets; research on college and professional women; and miscellaneous
     regional data sets.

Antonnuci, Toni, Nancy Gillett and Frances W. Hoyer. Values and Self-
     Esteem in Three Generations of Men and Women. JOURNAL OF
     GERONTOLOGY. 34(3):415-422 (May 1979)

     Similarities and differences in values within families (30 males and
     30 females) across three generations were examined. Women rated
     ambition, education, and intelligence higher than men.

Appelbaum, Eileen. BACK TO WORK: DETERMINANTS OF WOMEN'S SUCCESSFUL
     RE-ENTRY. Boston, Auburn House Publishing Co., 1981. 141 pp.

     Discusses important factors in status positions of women re-entering
     paid work: socioeconomic origin, earlier jobs held, and education
     completed. Highlights the conflict for a married woman between
     children and paid employment. Predicts that the trend of married
     women into paid employment may slow down.

Archbold, Patricia G. Analysis of Parentcaring by Women. HOME HEALTH
    CARE SERVICES QUARTERLY. 3(2):5-26 (Summer 1982)

    "Parentcaring" is defined as "provision of needed services to func-
    tionally impaired elderly parents." This study was of the effect on
    30 parentcaring women of the care they gave to parents. These care-
    givers should be made aware of the increasing demands of such care as
    their own physical resources lessen, and they should be more alert to
    the limited in-house services available to help them.

Arens, Diana Antos. Widowhood and Well-Being: an Examination of Sex
    Differences Within a Causal Model. INTERNATIONAL JOURNAL OF AGING
    AND HUMAN DEVELOPMENT. 15(1):27-40 (1982-83)

    Data from the National Council on the Aging survey, "Myth and Reality
    of Aging in America," conducted by Louis Harris & Associates in 1975,
    were analyzed in a causal model to discern differences in the effects
    of widowhood on the well-being of older men and women.

Atchley, Robert C. Process of Retirement: Comparing Women and Men. In:
    Szinovacz, Maximiliane, ed. WOMEN'S RETIREMENT: POLICY IMPLICATIONS
    OF RECENT RESEARCH. Beverly Hills, California, Sage Publications,
    1982. pp. 153-168.

    Atchley feels the ideal (but not easily realizable) way to study the
    retirement process is over a 50-year period, following the same indi-
    viduals through their preretirement stage, the retirement transition
    period, and then into the much later postretirement period. In his
    much shorter time study here, the interviews were with representa-
    tive men and women in all the three stages (but not the same indi-
    viduals in each group), seeking their attitudes toward retirement and
    their life satisfaction at these stages. According to this study,
    women are more likely than men to plan never to retire or to retire
    late, their economic status often determining this decision. This
    suggests that financial planning and economic resources are important
    issues for women.

Atchley, Robert C. SOCIAL FORCES IN LATER LIFE: AN INTRODUCTION TO SOCIAL
    GERONTOLOGY. 3rd ed. Belmont, California, Wadsworth Publishing Co.,
    1980. 467 pp.

    Throughout the text and tables of this 3rd edition of a classic work,
    there are numerous statements and statistics presented by age/sex.
    The chapter headings indicate the breadth of the work: scope of
    social gerontology; social psychology of the aging individual; age
    changes in situational context; psychology of aging; changing social
    context of later life; health; finances; employment and retirement;
    death, dying, bereavement and widowhood; personal adaptation to
    aging; societal and general social responses to aging; social

inequality; economy; politics and government; community association; religion; family, friends and neighbors; and conclusion (including policy issues). The extensive bibliography (pp. 397-465) also indicates the chapters to which each reference is relevant.

Attwood, William. MAKING IT THROUGH MIDDLE AGE: NOTES WHILE IN TRANSIT. New York, Atheneum, 1982. 239 pp.

This is a "fun" book, one with no moral message. It is written by a man from a man's point of view, but by one sensitive to the female point of view. See chapters on "Sex," "Marriage," and "Children."

Babchuk, Nicholas, et al. Voluntary Associations of the Aged. JOURNAL OF GERONTOLOGY. 34(4):579-587 (July 1979)

Examination of the voluntary associations of elderly men and women, as to: extent to which they affiliate with groups; whether men are more likely to belong to groups than women; the specific types of organizations which attract older people; how often those with memberships attend meetings and their general level of participation. Three of the six tables are by sex. Contrary to expectations, women were significantly more active in voluntary groups than men.

Baker, Diane, et al. Mortality and Early Retirement. SOCIAL SECURITY BULLETIN. 45(12):3-10 (December 1982)

Compared the survival rates of persons claiming retired-worker benefits at age 62 with those who did not. The assumption was that those in the claimant group did so because of health problems. Women had higher survival rates than men, in the group claiming retired-worker benefits, but not very different from other insured women. Statistics by age/sex.

Ball, Robert M. RECOMMENDATIONS OF THE BIPARTISAN NATIONAL COMMISSION ON SOCIAL SECURITY REFORM. [Washington, D.C., February 1, 1983] 19 + 8 pp. Reproduction of typescript.

Robert Ball, in his capacity as appointee to the National Commission on Social Security Reform, appeared before the House Committee on Ways and Means, February 1, 1983, to present the recommendations of the bipartisan Commission. In attachment No. 1, "Supplementary Statement," he adds the recommendations of the members selected by the Democratic leadership of Congress with respect to "Long-Term Financing" and "Issues of Special Concern to Women." He comments that significant changes in women's roles in society and the economy have caused inequities and unintended results for women as Social Security beneficiaries and suggests that earnings sharing is the most promising approach to solving the Social Security problems of special concern to women.

Barrett, Carol J. and Karen M. Schneweis. Empirical Search for Stages of Widowhood. OMEGA. 11(2):97-104 (1980-1981)

Structured interviews with 193 widows, age 62 and over (part of a larger needs assessment survey of the elderly in Wichita, Kansas) were utilized to bear out or refute the theory that stages of adjustment to widowhood exist beyond the initial stage of grief (the first of six defined stages). Results of the interviews provided evidence that the stresses of widowhood persist for years after the spouse's death, but there was no confirmation of the existence of separate stages of adaptation.

Barrow, Georgia M. and Patricia Smith. AGING, THE INDIVIDUAL, AND SOCIETY. 2d ed. St. Paul, Minnesota, West Publishing Co., 1983. 477 pp.

This edition, as is the first, is about ageism and the way people are thought about, evaluated, and treated on the basis of their age. In the second edition, the authors have incorporated many new ideas and new findings in the light of the increased research in the several intervening years (1979-1983). Most of the text addresses older people, not distinguishing by sex, but in certain chapters, there is a separation: Social Bonds: Family and Friends (pp. 99-132); Finances (especially the section on special problems of aged women), (pp. 171-175); and Sexuality (pp. 278-296).

Beckman, Linda J. and Betsy Bosak Houser. Consequences of Childlessness on the Social-Psychological Well-Being of Older Women. JOURNAL OF GERONTOLOGY. 37(2):243-250 (March 1982)

Evidence from social gerontology finds little support for the view that childless women are less satisfied or have a lessened feeling of well-being than others generally, although widowed-childless older women did have a lower psychological well-being than did widowed mothers, especially if the childless widow is also Jewish, nonreligious, and without social support or satisfying social interactions.

Behling, John H., Keith M. Kilty and Sara A. Foster. Scarce Resources for Retirement Planning: A Dilemma for Professional Women. JOURNAL OF GERONTOLOGICAL SOCIAL WORK. 5(3):49-60 (Spring 1983)

Little is known about female professional workers and the problems they experience with pre-retirement planning. This study surveyed 218 professional women as to their retirement plans, and compared their responses to those of 239 professional men, focusing on: 1) what resources are available to professional women as compared to men; 2) how gender is related to financial planning among professionals; and 3) how gender is related to expectations about retirement income. In general, women are disadvantaged in all these areas of research, and more should be done to meet their pre-retirement needs.

Benokraitis, Nijole. EMPLOYMENT PATTERNS OF DISPLACED HOMEMAKERS: AN EXPLORATORY STUDY. Baltimore, Maryland, University of Baltimore, Department of Sociology, March 1981. 72 pp.

Study based on interviews with 91 displaced homemakers to examine the job characteristics, job entry/re-entry processes and perceptions of important job attributes of a group of older workers/displaced homemakers, and to determine the relationship between variables and the current employment status of displaced homemakers. Following a detailed description of the study and its results, a final section discusses possible applications.

Benson, Helene A. WOMEN AND PRIVATE PENSIONS. Washington, D.C., Government Printing Office, 1980. 11 pp.

Employment patterns of women determine their private pensions. Some factors are fewer women working where no pension plans exist and low wages. ERISA and changing patterns of work may ease things for women. Although ERISA makes no distinction between male and female, it has improved the situation where a break in service occurs--even improved the special problems of divorcees. Overall, elderly women still live below the poverty level.

Berardo, Felix M., ed. Middle and Late Life Transitions. ANNALS OF THE AMERICAN ACADEMY OF POLITICAL AND SOCIAL SCIENCE, Vol. 464. November 1982. 187 pp.

The current preoccupation with the transitions of middle and old age has evolved from several historical, economic, and demographic changes, namely shifting of the population toward the middle of the age structure, and producing new stages in the life cycle, including long-term survival, the empty nest period, universal retirement, and an extended term of widowhood in late life. Several articles in this collection comment on women separately from men, and three are addressed quite directly to women (and are abstracted separately in this bibliography): Angela M. O'Rand and J.C. Henretta, "Women at Middle Age: Developmental Transitions;" Gordon F. Streib and Madeline Haug Penna, "Anticipating Transitions: Possible Options in 'Family' Forms;" and Boaz Kahana and Eva Kahana, "Clinical Issues of Middle Age and Later Life."

Berger, Raymond M. Unseen Minority: Older Gays and Lesbians. SOCIAL WORK. 27(3):236-242 (May 1982)

Informs social workers of the needs--legal, institutional, emotional and medical--of older homosexuals who are at present often ignored, especially the female.

Berkun, Cleo S. Changing Appearance for Women in the Middle Years of Life: Trauma? In: Markson, Elizabeth W., ed. OLDER WOMEN: ISSUES AND PROSPECTS. Lexington, Massachusetts, Lexington Books; D.C. Heath & Co., 1983. pp. 11-35.

The white middle-class woman today, at mid-life, can anticipate twenty-five more years of life, relatively child-free, healthy, and vigorous. But precisely at about this stage in her life, Berkun finds, she begins to accept the stigma of "aging" with its commonly accepted negative connotations as to her sexuality, her looks, her work, and her status in the world. As long as the public stress on youth as more acceptable than middle-age continues, the mature woman cannot throw off this stigma. If she has always been preoccupied with her apperance, the dilemma prevails. But if she goes too far in changing her traditional feminine role and discards old patterns of thought and behavior, she may feel uncertain and deviant. She may cling to an unwanted marriage, knowing the opportunities to contract another are slim. These problems may stand in the way of her "self-actualization" and the discovery of her real mid-life personality.

Block, Marilyn R., ed. DIRECTION OF FEDERAL LEGISLATION AFFECTING WOMEN OVER FORTY. College Park, Maryland, National Policy Center on Women and Aging, University of Maryland, 1982. 162 pp.

A compilation of Federal legislation over the past 50 years that has implications for the woman over 40. The legislation is identified and described in seven categories (by chapter): health; mental health; employment and training; educational opportunities; income maintenance; housing; and transportation, energy, crime and victimization. Each law is discussed "in terms of general intent, specific provision to achieve intent, and benefits and inequities imposed upon older women as a result of the law." Appendix A gives the Older Americans Act of 1965 as amended 1981 in Public Law 97-115. An introduction by Block discusses public policy on the older woman and gives general demographics, including women by cohorts.

Block, Marilyn R., Donald E. Gelfand and Nurit G. Golding. HEALTH CONCERNS OF OLDER WOMEN. College Park, Maryland, National Policy Center on Women and Aging, University of Maryland, 1983. 87 pp.

Health issues rank among the first three concerns of older Americans in most surveys, because they fear losing functional ability due to illness. This paper examines the health issues most important to the older woman, efforts on their part to meet those needs, and the differences among sub-groups of older women both as to health status and their utilization patterns of health care services. In Ch. 4, "Health Care Policy," 18 policy options are outlined for education and training, research, care and treatment, and cost containment.

Block, Marilyn R. Professional Women: Work Pattern as a Correlate of
Retirement Satisfaction. In: Szinovacz, Maximiliane, ed. WOMEN'S
RETIREMENT: POLICY IMPLICATIONS OF RECENT RESEARCH. Beverly Hills,
California, Sage Publications, 1982. pp. 183-194.

Differences in adjustment to retirement between men and women are
seldom discussed in gerontological literature, perhaps because of the
feeling that work is not a primary role for women, even during their
work years. Questionnaires were mailed to alumnae of the University
of Maryland (not necessarily a representative group). Results support the assumption that, in general, continuous work is associated
with higher retirement satisfaction, but that health, post-retirement
income, and retirement planning are additional factors in the satisfaction of women with retirement. Author recommends retirement
planning programs for the preretirement years as a very necessary
factor in elevating retirement satisfaction.

Block, Marilyn R., Janice L. Davidson and Jean D. Grambs. WOMEN OVER
FORTY: VISIONS AND REALITIES. New York, Springer Publishing Co.,
1981. 157 pp. (Springer Series: Focus on Women, Vol. 4)

Factual presentation of the research on older women, challenging
myths and stereotypes. Although intended primarily for students in
gerontology, human development, and women's studies courses, this
volume may also be used in related courses focusing on general
aspects of social or psychological understanding. Block points out
that academic emphasis on the older woman should result in increased
research. The Introduction and Ch. 1 give demographic profiles of
several facets of the older woman. Succeeding chapters present text,
with generous statistics on images of the older woman; menopause;
mental health; life situations (socialization, living arrangements,
changing life patterns), family life cycle and changes; employment and
retirement; ethnic and racial variations (including ethnic groups not
often reported on in the literature); and research issues. In this
last chapter, they re-emphasize that gerontological literature has
not focused to a large degree on the female aging process, and that
the literature reflects the "paucity" of research in the physiological, psychological, and sociological changes that occur in the middle
and later years. Fourteen page bibliography at end.

Boles, William and Hollye Jackson. Why Mary Cannot Afford Her Utility
Bills: an Evaluation of a Strategy to Promote Energy Conservation for
Low-Income Older Women Using Low-Cost and No-Cost Resources. JOURNAL
OF APPLIED GERONTOLOGY, 1:67-78 (June 1982)

An educational program on conservation of energy was undertaken.
Nevertheless, low-income women were found unable to reduce their
energy use much because: 1) they were already using as little as
they could, and 2) the insulation standards of the HUD buildings
where they lived were not energy saving. They put little credence
in government or energy company educational programs. Additionally,
utility rate structures favor larger use of energy.

Borenstein, Audrey. OLDER WOMEN IN 20th-CENTURY AMERICA: A SELECTED AND
    ANNOTATED BIBLIOGRAPHY. New York, Garland Publishing, Inc., 1982.
    351 pp. (Women's Studies Facts and Issues, Vol. 3)

In addition to titles on socio-economic issues, general gerontology,
and creativity, there are six sections (out of the total 16) on:
autobiographies, literature and aging, novels and novellas by and
about older women, oral histories, personal documents of older women,
and short stories by and about older women. Some classics are analyzed
in which both sexes are treated without highlighting either sex. There
are 885 citations (ranging from 1900-1982) with ample annotations, chosen
on the sound and modern premise that there is a "vital connection between
the circumstances, experiences, and perspective of a woman in her forties
and fifties with her life and thought in the decades that follow," and
that useful information about "older women" is concealed in much general
gerontological research.

Bradford, Leland P. and Martha I. Bradford. RETIREMENT: COPING WITH
    EMOTIONAL UPHEAVALS. Chicago, Nelson-Hall, 1979. 202 pp.

The authors, professionals in psychology and behavioral science,
on their own retirement, found themselves facing adaptation to this
new life stage. The book recounts this experience, beginning first
with Leland's and then with Martha's conception of the problems of
recognizing and understanding the emotional upheavals of retirement.
The remainder of the book speaks to a wife's reactions and adjustments, or to a husband's, or to the common joint adjustments, either
their own, or those of other retired singles or couples retired or
planning to retire. It is Martha's feelings, experiences and adjustments which interest us in this psychological treatment of
retirement.

Braito, Rita and Donna Anderson. The Ever-Single Elderly Woman. In:
    Markson, Elizabeth W., ed. OLDER WOMEN: ISSUES AND PROSPECTS:
    Lexington, Massachusetts, Lexington Books; D.C. Heath & Co., 1983.
    pp. 195-225.

Identifies what is known about the ever-single elderly woman in our
society, typically a very small portion of the entire population, but
a proportion which now seems to be increasing, especially as singlehood becomes a viable alternative to marriage. Notwithstanding,
marriage and remarriage remain the norm. Ever-single women are a
"diverse population," about which we lack information on how they
cope with living in a status other than that of the marital norm.
Author reviews the available literature and gives a description of
the ever-single woman as to her: education; income; health; social
life; housing; work and retirement; and life satisfaction. Short
discussions on rural and black ever-singles. Six pages of references
appended.

Branch, Laurence G. and Alan M. Jette. Framingham Disability Study, Pt. I,
Social Disability Among the Aging. AMERICAN JOURNAL OF PUBLIC
HEALTH. 71(11):1202-1210 (November 1981). Questionnaire on social
disability at end. Also: Pt. II, Physical Disability Among the Aging,
by Alan M. Jette and Laurence G. Branch. Ibid., pp. 1211-1216.

Social disability was defined as dependence due to problems in housekeeping, transportation, social interaction, food preparation, and
shopping. Women more than men believe those needs are not well met
and that age increases the difficulties. On the physical side, comparison is made with earlier studies on six daily activities. Women
75 and over in the Framingham sample seem more handicapped than men,
but this is not yet determined for America as a whole. Tables by
sex.

Brebner, Ruth A. and Sharon K. Sundre. Deciders, Explorers, Dabblers,
Evaders: Women in Career Development Transition. LIFELONG LEARNING:
THE ADULT YEARS. 6(4):14-15,23,26 (December 1982)

Describes a program in Minneapolis, "Career Development for Women,"
which assists women, young and old, to develop skills to meet their
special needs. Four types of women are identified and suggestions
made to help each type secure appropriate employment.

Brickfield, C.F. Women in Their Later Years: a Time of New Challenges.
In: International Conference of Social Gerontology, 9th, Quebec,
August 27-28, 1980. ADAPTABILITY AND AGING, Vol. 2. Paris,
International Center of Social Gerontology, May 1981. pp. 43-48.

Author states that older women, like younger women, want to have more
positive control over the forces that shape their lives. He discusses
the very visible changes that have been taking place in the United
States as they affect the lives of middle aged and older women, and
the needs and challenges of these women today.

Brody, Elaine M. Women in the Middle and Family Help to Older People.
GERONTOLOGIST. 21(5):471-480 (October 1981)

Discussion of middle-aged women, in the middle family generation, who
have added the care of older dependent family members to their traditional job of homemaker and their emerging additional outside role as
paid employee.

Brown, Eileen T. Theories of Adult Personality Development and Socializa-
tion: Toward an Understanding of Midlife Transitions in Women. In:
Raynor, Joel O., et al. MOTIVATION, CAREER STRIVING AND AGING.
Washington, D.C., Hemisphere Publishing Corp., 1982. pp. 331-352.

Discusses the psychological aspects of midlife woman, and analyzes
the causes of midlife changes. Author notes that this woman is more
depressed than at other ages, in part the result of having been educated
for a career outside the home, and then having entered the traditional
career of marriage, wife and mother.

Brubaker, Timothy H. and Charles B. Hennon. Responsibility for Household
    Tasks: Comparing Dual-Earner and Dual-Retired Marriages. In:
    Szinovacz, Maximiliane, ed. WOMEN'S RETIREMENT: POLICY IMPLICATIONS
    OF RECENT RESEARCH. Beverly Hills, California, Sage Publications,
    1982. pp. 205-219.

    As wives of the dual-earner married couples retire, the husbands have
    normally already retired, making them dual-retired couples. This
    study of 207 dual-earners and dual-retired marriages examines the
    perceived actual and expected division of household responsibilities
    and provides information on these arrangements from the female
    perspective. The discrepancies between behavior and expectations
    found in this study may represent a major source of marital conflict
    among such couples. The findings have policy implications for prere-
    tirement programs, community education, marriage and family
    counseling.

Burkhauser, Richard V. and Karen C. Holden, eds. CHALLENGE TO SOCIAL SECURITY:
    THE CHANGING ROLES OF WOMEN AND MEN IN AMERICAN SOCIETY. New York,
    Academic Press, 1982. 272 pp.

    Adjustments of the Social Security system to changes in the roles of women
    and men in present society should be preceded by open discussion of speci-
    fic reforms and the ensuing financing. In this collection of articles,
    specialists present the inequities of the present Social Security system
    (especially toward women as homemakers, widows, divorcees, or as workers)
    and suggest reforms (or oppose them) and changes in income which would
    result (again especially for aged women). Financing of reforms is
    discussed.

Burkhauser, Richard V. and Joseph Quinn. THE RELATIONSHIP BETWEEN MANDATORY
    RETIREMENT AGE LIMITS AND PENSION RULES IN THE RETIREMENT DECISION.
    Washington, D.C., Urban Institute, 1981. 111 pp. (Urban Institute
    Research Paper 1348-03)

    Analyzes how raising the mandatory retirement age limits affects the
    labor market. Some text and several tables by sex.

Burkhead, Dan L. Lifetime Earnings Estimates for Men and Women in the
    United States: 1979. CURRENT POPULATION REPORTS, Series P-60
    (CONSUMER INCOME), No. 139, February 1979. 37 pp.

    This report differs from earlier ones in that its estimates now take
    into account the in- and out-character of the participation of women
    (18-64) in the work force. The lifetime earnings estimates presented
    here are the expected or average amounts based on cross-sectional
    earnings data by age, sex, and educational attainment for the years
    1978, 1979, 1980, data from these three years being averaged in order
    to obtain a sample size large enough to support this study. The report
    is important for women, even allowing for assumptions which the author
    had to apply to the data, assumptions which understandably impose some
    limitations on the results reached.

Burks, Jayne Buress. Economic Crises for Women: Aging and Retirement
      Years. In: Quadnago, Jill S. AGING, THE INDIVIDUAL AND SOCIETY:
      READINGS IN SOCIAL GERONTOLOGY. New York, St. Martin's Press, 1980.
      pp. 455-468.

      Highlights the in- and out-participation of women in the labor force
      with consequent limitations in pay, retirement income, Social Security
      and other pensions.

Butler, Frieda R. RESOURCE GUIDE ON BLACK AGING. Washington, D.C.,
      Institute for Urban Affairs and Research, Howard University, 1981.
      167 pp.

      Brief one or two pages of text on a wide variety of aspects of aged
      blacks, accompanied by some tables and bibliographies. In the tables
      for employment, life expectancy, persons surviving to a specified
      age, and attitudes, data are by age/sex.

Butler, Robert N. Health Issues, Aging Research and Aging Women. HOT FLASH:
      NEWSLETTER FOR MIDDLE AND OLDER WOMEN, 1(4):1,6 (Spring/Summer 1982)

      This is a precis of the keynote address of Dr. Robert Butler to the
      April 1981 Stony Brook Conference on "Health Issues of Older Women:
      A Projection to the Year 2000." Dr. Butler pointed out that
      increasingly the problems of aging will be those of women. This
      poses problems for research, especially about women, and for the edu-
      cation of those planning a career in geriatrics.

Cain, Leonard D. The Impact of Manhart on Pension Payments and the Legal Status
      of the Elderly. AGING AND WORK. 2(3):147-159 (Summer 1979)

      The U.S. Supreme Court Manhart decision rules out unequal pension
      contributions based on sex-segregated life expectancy tables
      ("elderly" are both men and women), but raises other issues yet to be
      addressed.

Cameron, Colin, comp. THE DISPLACED HOMEMAKER: A BIBLIOGRAPHY. Monticello,
      Illinois, Vance Bibliographies, January 1982. 48 pp. (Vance Biblio-
      graphies, Public Administration Series Bibliography P-895)

      Bibliography is arranged in the following categories: widowed,
      divorced, or separated; health matters; displaced homemakers and
      single heads of families; economic and financial aspects; readying
      for employment; on the job; discrimination at the workplace; legisla-
      tion; networking; programs; research, studies, government analyses
      and statistics; bibliographies, sources, resources and directories;
      films; and addresses.

Campbell, Shirley. Delayed Mandatory Retirement and the Working Woman.
     GERONTOLOGIST. 19(3):257-263 (June 1979)

     The effect of the changes in the laws concerning mandatory retirement
     on working women and the impact of this on the economy.

Cape, Ronald D.T. and Philip J. Henschke. Perspective of Health in Old
     Age. JOURNAL OF THE AMERICAN GERIATRICS SOCIETY. 28(3):295-299
     (July 1980)

     A group of 385 elderly subjects was studied to assess their degree of
     disability, consumption of drugs, and need for health care. Tables
     by sex.

Carp, Frances M. and Abraham Carp. The Ideal Residential Area. RESEARCH
     ON AGING. 4(4):411-439 (December 1982)

     This research was conducted in two studies, one to reveal ideal resi-
     dential characteristics if a large group of individuals, 25 years and
     older, were to consider moving, and the other, the ways in which
     older women (90 of them) would describe the ideal residential
     situation. The importance of esthetic qualities was strong at all
     ages. With respect to access to 15 different services and facili-
     ties, none were desired in the same block as the residence; access to
     schools and transportation was less desired by older women, but
     "walking distance" to basic services was considered by them to be
     desirable.

Carr-Ruffino, Norma. THE PROMOTABLE WOMAN: BECOMING A SUCCESSFUL MANAGER.
     Belmont, California, Wadsworth Publishing Co., 1982. 473 pp.

     Sets down in orderly fashion the knowledge of attitudes and skills a woman
     must have to be promotable and become a successful manager. These quali-
     ties are as essential for the older woman entering or re-entering the
     labor market as for a younger one. An appendix contains networks of
     women's organizations.

Catalyst. WHEN CAN YOU START? THE COMPLETE JOB-SEARCH GUIDE FOR WOMEN OF
     ALL AGES. New York, Macmillan Publishing Co., 1981. 148 pp.

     An innovative, practical guide to every stage of job hunting. Describes
     a woman's legal rights when job-hunting and includes information on how to
     become aware of rewarding jobs; writing resumes; interviewing, accepting
     or rejecting job offers. Ch. 4, "Ways and Means" gives 15 approaches to
     job-hunting. Lists organizations and agencies, pp. 123-124; bibliography,
     pp. 125-128; Catalyst's network of career resources centers, pp. 129-148.

Catholic University of America. Center for the Study of Pre-Retirement and
Aging. SYMPOSIUM ON OLDER AMERICANS OF EURO-ETHNIC ORIGIN. Washington,
D.C., [1980?]. 90 pp.

The Symposium felt that the problems of aging are really economic
problems, and undertook to demonstrate its point of view. See especially
the sections, "Older Women: Policy Recommendations for the 1980's" and
"White Ethnic Women in Their Later Years." Elderly women, the fastest
growing segment of the American population, must learn to live independently despite any handicaps from ethnicity, ill-health, poverty and
societal loss. Divorced or never married women are less susceptible to
these dilemmas. Symposium agreed that future national policy for older
women needs to involve both the public and private sectors of our economy.

Cauhape, Elizabeth. FRESH STARTS: MEN AND WOMEN AFTER DIVORCE. New York,
Basic Books, Inc., Publishers, 1983. 338 pp.

A book about upwardly mobile professional men and women with origins in
the middle, lower-middle, and working classes who are involved, at midlife, in divorce, one of the powerful crises in middle age in which the
divorcing individuals sense great disruption to their former life-style.
The author describes the range of new life-style options open to them, and
how they may assess the options, especially in terms of their social
resources. Her research suggests there are some eight different specific
aftermaths (choices or options) in post-divorce. She finds that many men
and women do better than expected, finding themselves happier in post-
divorce than in pre-divorce, and using the crisis as an impetus to new
personal growth. While the author considers the problems and solutions of
both men and women, the text and the examples illustrate the separateness
of the issues, so that the reader has a definite picture of those of the
mature woman. A fourteen-page bibliography is appended.

Chan, Teresita and Donald G. Fowles. THE OLDER WORKER. Washington, D.C.,
U.S. Government Printing Office, 1980. 35 pp. (Statistical Reports
on Older Americans, No. 6)

Statistical reports and tables on selected characteristics of older
workers in such areas as race, marital status, education, industry, occupation, part-time work, self-employment, unemployment, and desire to work.
All tables by sex/age.

Cherlin, Andrew. A Sense of History: Recent Research on Aging and the Family.
In: Hess, Beth B. and Kathleen Bond, eds. LEADING EDGES: RECENT RESEARCH
ON PSYCHOLOGICAL AGING. Washington, D.C., U.S. Government Printing
Office, 1981. pp. 21-49.

Cherlin notes that earlier students of the contemporary family paid little
attention to history, and most historians paid little attention to the
family, a research attitude that by the 1960s had begun to change with
historians discovering the family, and family sociologists discovering
history. An important new body of research on family life began to appear

by the 1970s. The author summarizes these recent developments and discusses their implications for the family relations of the men and women who will be entering old age in the near future. He specifically addresses the older woman in the sub-sections on: divorce and remarriage; and women's labor force participation. This is reprinted in: Riley, Matilda White, Beth B. Hess and Kathleen Bond, eds. AGING IN SOCIETY: SELECTED REVIEWS OF RECENT RESEARCH. Hillsdale, New Jersey, Lawrence Erlbaum Associates, Publishers, 1983. pp. 5-23.

Chiriboga, David A. Adaptation to Marital Separation in Later and Earlier Life. JOURNAL OF GERONTOLOGY. 37(1):109-114 (January 1982)

In this research (including long-time married but recently separated women) there were 125 men and 185 women ranging in age from 20-79. The major hypothesis of the study was that the older persons would show greater evidence of psychosocial disruption, and the research sustained that hypothesis. Men and women have different vulnerabilities. Text discussion is separated by sex.

Chirikos, Thomas N. and Gilbert Nestel. Economic Consequences of Poor Health in Mature Women. In: Shaw, Lois B., ed. UNPLANNED CAREERS: THE WORKING LIVES OF MIDDLE-AGED WOMEN. Lexington, Massachusetts, Lexington Books, 1982. pp. 93-108.

The economic consequences of poor health appear to be more severe for women than for men of the same age. Women are more likely than men to report being work-disabled. Even if they remain in the labor force, women reduce their working hours more drastically and experience more unemployment in response to health conditions, all of which reduces their already low wages/income. About 60% of white women without impaired health are likely to be in the labor force. Probably about 66% of black women without impaired health are in the labor force. The participation of white women is reduced by 12% if moderately impaired, 24% if substantially impaired, and 57% if severely impaired. Parallel statistics for black women are 12%, 25%, and 62%.

Chirikos, Thomas N. SEX AND RACE DIFFERENTIALS IN ECONOMIC CONSEQUENCES OF POOR HEALTH. Columbus, Ohio State University, Center for Human Resource Research, March 1982. 62 pp.

The principal objective of this study of men and women (younger and older than 50) was to obtain a better understanding of the relation of health (earlier and current) to labor market behavior, specifically hours lost and lower wage rates, of white and black men and women. It was found that the record for whites and blacks is not the same, and that they are again different for men and women of each race. Data are from the "National Longitudinal Survey of the Labor Market Experience of Mature Men and Women." Many of the tables are by sex and age.

Cicirelli, Victor G. HELPING ELDERLY PARENTS: THE ROLE OF ADULT CHILDREN.
Boston, Massachusetts, Auburn House Publishing Co., 1981. 199 pp.

Today, middle-aged adult children continue to help their elderly parents
(as they have traditionally done), making it possible for them to remain
in their own homes, stay out of institutional care, or live in the home of
the adult children. This book primarily looks into how these adult
children feel about their caregiving assistance, reporting on interviews
with 164 middle-aged adult children (75 men and 89 women) caring for one
or two aged parents. Only in Ch. 4 (pp. 59-64), where the participants are
described, are elderly mothers singled out for discussion.

Coalition on Women and the Budget. INEQUALITY OF SACRIFICE: THE IMPACT OF
THE REAGAN BUDGET ON WOMEN. Washington, D.C., National Women's Law
Center, 1983. 82 pp.

The ad hoc Coalition on Women and the Budget came together in 1982 to ana-
lyze the fiscal year 1983 budget, and found that women, especially the
poorest women, were being asked to shoulder a disproportionate share of
the country's economic burden. The Report considers the impact of various
Federal programs on women of all ages. The section on "Older Women"
(pp. 56-71) cites many statistics in presenting the impact on older women
of reduced funding of: 1) Senior Community Service Employment Program; 2)
Jobs Training Partnership Act; 3) Social Security; 4) Supplemental
Security Income; 5) Medicare and Medicaid; 6) Food Stamps; 7) Housing
programs; 8) Low-Income Energy Assistance Program; 9) Older Americans Act
Nutrition Program.

Cohler, Bertram J., Henry U. Grunebaum and Donna Moran Robbins. MOTHERS,
GRANDMOTHERS, AND DAUGHTERS: PERSONALITY AND CHILDCARE IN THREE-GENERATION
FAMILIES. New York, John Wiley & Sons, 1981. 456 pp.

Among adult relationships, that between the mother of young children and
her own mother is perhaps the most complex. Here are case studies of four
such mothers and grandmothers (living together or in close proximity)
which illustrate the psychological significance of such contacts and
mutual supports. The study describes the continuing personality development and adult socialization of these urban Italo-American women in their
intergenerational continuity. Four of the chapters describe the individual members of the families and characterize in depth the personality of
each, the extent and quality of the contacts, and a retrospective account
of the grandmother's experience in rearing her own daughter. The findings
of the study are described: 1) nature and extent of contact across
generations; 2) impact of these relations on the psychological development
of the interviewees; and 3) the transmission of family themes across
generations. The last chapter returns to the members of these families
four years later, with an updating of their lives, problems and solutions.
Bibliography: pp. 365-402.

Cohler, Bertram J. Stress or Support: Relations Between Older Women From Three European Ethnic Groups and Their Relatives. In: Manuel, Ron C., ed., MINORITY AGING. Westport, Connecticut, Greenwood Press, 1982. pp. 115-120.

Close-knit family and neighborhood life in which cultural traditions are preserved is considered additionally to reduce the impact of otherwise stressful life events. Less attention has been paid to the anomaly that the maintenance of such relationships might in itself provoke strain and related problems in the older woman.

Cole, Katherine W., ed. MINORITY ORGANIZATIONS: A NATIONAL DIRECTORY. 2d ed. Garrett Park, Maryland, Garrett Park Press, 1982. 814 pp.

The directory is arranged alphabetically by organization, but in the very detailed subject index, under terms beginning "Women's," there are numerous citations to women's organizations divided by Black, Hispanic, Minorities (general), and Native American. A perusal of these organizations will indicate which ones relate to, or specifically include, the older woman in their interest field.

Colman, Vanda, et al. TILL DEATH DO US PART: CAREGIVING WIVES OF SEVERELY DISABLED HUSBANDS. Oakland, California, Older Women's League, 1982. 18 pp.

Discusses the plight of wives who assume total care of their severely disabled husbands, frequently over a long period of time. Points out the present paucity of home care services and financial aid available to them, since health insurance and Medicare mostly pay for care in the hospital and in nursing homes. Suggests support services such as visiting nurses, mutual support groups, respite weekends, and adult day care, which are currently available (but not widely so) to these caregiving wives.

Colvez, Alain and Madeleine Blanchet. Disability Trends in the United States Population, 1966-76: Analysis of Reported Causes. AMERICAN JOURNAL OF PUBLIC HEALTH. 71(5):456-471 (May 1981)

In the 1966-1976 decade, the disability reports increased definitely in numbers. For women 65+ in age, the increase was associated with diabetes and circulatory diseases (exclusive of heart conditions and hypertension). Two of the four tables are by sex/age.

Cool, Linda and Justine McCabe. The "Scheming Hag" and the "Dear Old Thing": the Anthropology of Aging Women. In: Sokolovsky, Jay, ed. GROWING OLD IN DIFFERENT SOCIETIES. Belmont, California, Wadsworth Publishing Co., 1983. pp. 56-63.

The authors suggest that no one entity can be called "the aged," due to sociocultural as well as sexual variation. In this first article of its kind, anthropologists Cool and McCabe cross-culturally explore late adulthood from the female perspective, and attempt to go further than the simple view that older women are either hateful "scheming hags" or kindly "dear old things." They contrast the U.S. themes of the depressed middle-aged or older woman and the leveling of sex-role differences with the themes of growing dominance and power and role reversal of older women in many nonindustrial societies. One section is on "The Paradox of the Aging American Woman" and the other on "The Aging Woman in Mediterranean Society" (the latter based on two Mediterranean societies where female subordination prevails). They conclude that women, like men, are products (and producers) of the particular culture in which they are socialized and live out their lives.

Cooper, Pamela E. Subjective Time Experience in an Intergenerational Sample. INTERNATIONAL JOURNAL OF AGING AND HUMAN DEVELOPMENT. 13(3):183-193 (1981)

The roles chronological age and gender play in subjective time experience. Findings by sex.

Costello, Mary T. and John A. Meacham. Sex Differences in Perception of Aging. INTERNATIONAL JOURNAL OF AGING AND HUMAN DEVELOPMENT. 12(4): 283-290 (1980-1981)

Extension of an earlier report on perception of aging through assessing sex differences and by focusing on specific events of aging for each sex rather than global perception. The study re-confirmed an earlier finding that aging is perceived as less difficult for oneself than for others, but the question of whether aging is more difficult for women than for men is too general for a clear answer, only really measureable for specific events.

Cross, K. Patricia. ADULTS AS LEARNERS. San Francisco, Jossey-Bass, Publishers, 1981. 300 pp.

The author uses UNESCO's definition of "lifelong education and learning" and applies it to adults and to the present resources of education. She writes particularly of the problems in women's lives (changing roles, opening up of opportunities, self-doubt, further education) which must be met by those who plan for the education of the elderly.

Crossman, Linda, Cecilia London and Clemmie Barry. Older Women Caring for Disabled Spouses: A Model of Supportive Services. GERONTOLOGIST. 21(5):464-470 (October 1981)

Description of a multi-service support program for older women caring for disabled husbands at home. Also recommendations for further study.

Crosson, Carrie W. and Elizabeth A. Robertson-Tchabo. Age and Preference for Complexity Among Manifestly Creative Women. HUMAN DEVELOPMENT. 26(3): 149-155 (May/June 1983)

This research involved 271 "manifestly creative women" (23-87 years of age) and a control group of 76 women (26-74 years of age) not selected for creativity. Results of measurement by creativity scales showed no loss of creativity with age among the 271 creative women, but significant loss among the 76 not selected for creativity. The importance of selecting a homogeneous sample is stressed, and questions concerning the value of creative attributes for successful aging were raised.

Crystal, Stephen. AMERICA'S OLD AGE CRISIS: PUBLIC POLICY AND THE TWO WORLDS OF AGING. New York, Basic Books, Inc., Publishers, 1982. 232 pp.

Using new survey data, the author gives a comprehensive account of the changing needs of the elderly and what this means for health care, pensions, Social Security, and other programs. Ch. 2 touches briefly on the demography of women, their changing circumstances and needs and decline in poverty. Ch. 3 touches, again briefly, on their living arrangements, especially as influenced by widowhood (p. 40-41). In Ch. 5, brief mention is made of the disparity in pension coverage and vesting, between men and women, and the resulting pension income (p. 117-119). In Ch. 6, on the growth of the welfare state, women are treated to a page and a half of comment with respect to income from Supplementary Security Income and from Social Security itself (pp. 151-152). Statistics accompany most of these statements.

Cuellar, Jose B., E. Percil Stanford and Danielle I. Miller-Soule. UNDERSTAND-ING MINORITY AGING: PERSPECTIVES AND SOURCES. San Diego, California, Center on Aging, College of Human Services, San Diego State University, 1982. 379 pp.

This is the product of the Minority Aging Codification Project of the San Diego State University, where to date some 1500 literature references have been made available to researchers in minority aging (majority of this material is found in the Center on Aging). First section of the report consists of a history of the Codification Project; minority aging research; minority aging policy; five signed chapters on various minority groups; and a cross-cultural summary and conclusions. These subject treatments are general, and address women specifically very little. The second part of the report consists of five bibliographies arranged by minority groups, plus a section of "uncodified references." There is no breakdown which would present literature on aged women in minorities, and the searcher must look for them throughout the several arrangements by author. This method is tedious but productive, especially of otherwise fugitive materials.

Cunningham, Phyllis M. Status of Women. In: Klevins, Chester, ed. MATERIALS & METHODS IN ADULT AND CONTINUING EDUCATION. Los Angeles, Klevens Publications, Inc., 1982. (Materials and Methods Series) pp. 43-51.

Cunningham joins earlier researchers in believing that mature women (35+ in age) will continue to be urged by social conditions to return for further education. She discusses who they are, their numbers, and their needs which an institution should meet, including curriculum changes and counseling. She goes so far as to predict that survival for many educational institutions in the next decade may depend on their ability to adapt to the changing needs of students.

Davidson, Janice L. EMPLOYMENT CONCERNS OF OLDER WOMEN. College Park, Maryland, National Policy Center on Women and Aging, University of Maryland, 1983. 77 pp.

Describes five basic areas related to the employment concerns of older women: 1) economic status; 2) labor force participation; 3) as workers; 4) employment needs and opportunities; and 5) employment policy options. The policy options are analyzed according to equity, adequacy, coherence, cost, feasibility, and latent consequences.

Davidson, Janice L. Issues of Employment and Retirement in the Lives of Women Over Age 40. In: Osgood, Nancy J., ed. LIFE AFTER WORK: RETIREMENT, LEISURE, RECREATION, AND THE ELDERLY. New York, Praeger, 1982. pp. 95-118.

First section briefly outlines factors related to the economic status of older women. Second section describes changes in the role of work; sex, and age discrimination in the labor force; the nature of the work done by women; the variety of work histories and experiences within the population of women workers; and the needs and options of older women entering the work place.

Davis, Lenwood G. THE BLACK AGED IN THE UNITED STATES: AN ANNOTATED BIBLIOGRAPHY. Westport, Connecticut, Greenwood Press, 1980. 200 pp.

Annotated bibliography on the black aged divided into eight sections, two of which are by subject (Black Aged and Slavery, and Black Old Folks' Homes), with the remaining sections by form of material, subdivided by subject. The index, under the notation "Women," indicates pages on which articles on women are found (more than 30). This is not the totality of pertinent references, as more are scattered throughout the entire bibliography, and the reader will do well to scan all sections. One should keep in mind that the "aged black woman" is frequently younger than the "older white woman," given the difference in the life expectancy of the two groups.

Daymont, Thomas and Anne Statham. Occupational Atypicality: Changes, Causes, and Consequences. In: Shaw, Lois B., ed. UNPLANNED CAREERS: THE WORKING LIVES OF MIDDLE-AGED WOMEN. Lexington, Massachusetts, Lexington Books, 1982. pp. 61-76.

The authors found that middle-aged women tended to be working in "female-typed" occupations. To be in this type of employment, they found, was detrimental to women's blue-collar wages though this was not true of women in white-collar employment. Family responsibilities explained much of the earnings differential for women not in atypical work, but for the older women these responsibilities were not the major reason for remaining in "female-typed" work.

Dement, William C., Laughton E. Miles and Mary A. Carskadon. "White Paper" on
Sleep and Aging. JOURNAL OF THE AMERICAN GERIATRICS SOCIETY. 30(1):25-50
(January 1982)

Investigates problems of sleep and wakefulness. First half of the paper
is on "Complaints and Their Meaning: Subjective and Objective Measures of
Sleep in Elderly Men and Women." The authors suggest the kind of future
research that would contribute to the well-being of older people, most of
whom seem, generally, to be dissatisfied with their sleep. Appended is a
comprehensive bibliography on sleep and aging. (338 references).

Depner, Charlene and Berit Ingersoll. Employment Status and Social Support: The
Experience of the Mature Woman. In: Szinovacz, Maximiliane, ed. WOMEN'S
RETIREMENT: POLICY IMPLICATIONS OF RECENT RESEARCH. Beverly Hills,
California, Sage Publications, 1982. pp. 61-75.

The authors believe the social support resources of a working woman during
her labor force participation carry over into and affect her well-being in
her retirement years. Using data from a National Institute on Aging
"Supports of the Elderly" project survey, the authors carried out a
triangulation of comparisons, pointing up distinctive features of the
social support networks of retired women as compared with 1) retired men,
2) employed women, and 3) housewives. Retired women in general had a
larger social network and a larger inner circle of close relationships,
modified by their age, gender and earlier labor force participation.

DeShane, Michael R. and Keren B. Wilson. DIVORCE IN LATE LIFE: EMERGING
TRENDS AND PROBLEMS. Portland, Oregon, Portland State University,
Institute on Aging, November 1981. 139 pp. + 55 pp. of Survey
Questionnaire. Final report to the NRTA/AARP Andrus Foundation Grant.

This reports the findings from a 15-month extensive research effort into
the phenomenon of divorce in late life, a topic on which virtually nothing
is known. It is intended to be an initial description of the extent to
which divorce affects older persons. Section 1 (pp. 1-23) examines past
and present divorce rates and future prospects for older persons. Section
2 (pp. 24-49) examines the current legal, social and psychological status
of divorced older persons, with emphasis on those who are divorced before
age 60. Section 3 (pp. 50-121) represents the major thrust of the
research efforts, a survey of 81 divorcing older persons in two counties
of Oregon, describing that group, the legal process, and the impact of
divorce on social relationships and economic and psychological well-being
of those divorced in late life. The analysis does not go into the adaptation of divorcing older people to their new situation. A final section
discusses the conclusions reached and indicates areas of necessary further
research.

Dienstfrey, Harris and Joseph Lederer. WHAT DO YOU WANT TO BE WHEN YOU GROW
OLD? Toronto, Bantam Books, 1979. 301 pp.

The message of this book is that old age is a "time of choice and new
directions," not a time of waiting for death, a concept which modern

society, even medicine, is now prepared to accept. However, each person or couple must face his own kind of change. Useful suggstions for the older woman are found in "Traveling Woman," and "Working Woman." The last chapter, "You should Live So Long," also has a great deal of applicability to the older woman.

Dillingham, Alan E. Age and Workplace Injuries. AGING AND WORK. 4(1):1-10 (Winter 1981)

New evidence on the relationship between age and the incidence of workplace injuries analyzed in this study. Age-injury profiles for males and females compared and found similar when controlling for sex differences in the occupational distribution of employment.

Dissinger, Katherine. OLD, POOR, ALONE, AND HAPPY: HOW TO LIVE NICELY ON NEARLY NOTHING. Chicago, Nelson-Hall, 1980. 261 pp.

How a woman may develop coping techniques and solve problems peculiar to old age, poverty, and aloneness. Author makes valuable points and suggestions, particularly that of beginning early to plan for retirement, the better to assure a creative and happy one.

Dodson, Fitzhugh and Paula Reuben. HOW TO GRANDPARENT. New York, Harper and Row, Publishers, 1981. 290 pp.

This book by psychologists is in reality a "Dr. Spock for Grandparents," detailing the serious, interesting and rewarding role of being a grandparent. It points out rules and psychology of understanding and coping with the various special aspects through the young years of grandchildren. Grandparents are not differentiated by sex, but if grandmother can and wants to fill roles traditionally assigned to grandfather, and vice versa, the advice is equally applicable. Bibliography: pp. 278-282.

Doss, Martha Merrill, ed. DIRECTORY OF SPECIAL OPPORTUNITIES FOR WOMEN: A NATIONAL GUIDE OF EDUCATIONAL OPPORTUNITIES, CAREER INFORMATION NETWORKS, AND PEER COUNSELING ASSISTANCE FOR ENTRY OR REENTRY INTO THE WORK FORCE. Garrett Park, Maryland, Garrett Park Press, 1981. 243 pp.

Very practical directory guiding women (in traditional and in non-traditional fields) to the sources which will help her in life changes, including opportunities in paid employment, whether she is a younger or an older woman.

Drazga, Linda, Melinda Upp and Virginia Reno. Low-Income Aged: Eligibility and Participation in SSI. SOCIAL SECURITY BULLETIN. 45(5):28-35 (May 1982)

Evaluation of the Social Security Administration's (SSA) methods for estimating the number of persons eligible for Supplemental Security Income (SSI) payments. Among factors to be taken into account in determining

this eligibility are availability of State Supplements: population characteristics, including sex, race, and marital status; knowledge, experience,
and attitudes of those eligible for SSI but not participating; actions and
attitudes of local office personnel. Tables and discussion by sex.

Duncan, Theodore G., ed. OVER 55: A HANDBOOK ON HEALTH. Illustrated by Joyce
Richman. Philadelphia, Franklin Institute. Distributed by Charles
Scribner's Sons, 1982. 668 pp.

This handbook by 47 specialists addresses itself to the older woman in
two chapters: "Gynecological Problems" by Frank Gaudiano (pp. 229-239),
and "Sex After 55" by Edward T. Auer (pp. 435-442). In "Population
Trends" by D.J. Kolasky and S. Hoover (pp. 499-504); some statistics are
by sex.

Edwards, Willie M. and Francis Flynn, comps. GERONTOLOGY: A CROSS-NATIONAL
CORE LIST OF SIGNIFICANT WORKS. Ann Arbor, Michigan, Institute of
Gerontology, University of Michigan, 1982. 365 pp.

This imposing bibliography is a follow-up of their earlier compilation,
GERONTOLOGY: A CORE LIST OF SIGNIFICANT WORKS (Institute of Gerontology,
University of Michigan, 1978). In the present work, the additional new
titles include English-Language monographs from outside the United States,
i.e. Canada and the United Kingdom. These titles are listed by broad subject areas (such as demography, economics, education, employment, health,
history, housing and environments, etc.) and grouped thereunder by the
three geographic areas. An author and a title index accompany the
bibliography, but there is no detailed separate subject index to the
entire work. This would have been a definite aid on more particular or
defined subjects. Since there is no grouping under "Women," the
researcher can either examine the entire listing of titles for obvious
ones, or turn to a given general subject section and again select promising titles. In the subject arranged section on "Social Aspects," for
instance, out of the 139 monographs cited for the United States, 19 can be
identified just from the wording of the title as concerning women, with
imprints ranging from 1973-1980. Many of the citations with general
titles, on close examination, would undoubtedly be found to contain
valuable chapters or segments on the older woman.

Elder, Glen H., Jr. and Jeffrey K. Liker. Hard Times In Women's Lives: Historical
Influences Across Forty Years. AMERICAN JOURNAL OF SOCIOLOGY. 88(2):
241-269 (September 1982)

An analysis of the effect of the Great Depression on women born before
1910 who were of the middle or lower class. This period of "loss
adjustment" assisted their coping with other later losses in old age.
The adequacy of this coping was greater for the middle than the lower
class woman because of her better education and socio-economic status.

Employee Benefit Research Institute. BIBLIOGRAPHY OF RESEARCH: RETIREMENT INCOME AND CAPITAL ACCUMULATION PROGRAMS. Washington, D.C., 1981. Each section repaged. Looseleaf. To be updated with insertions.

This annotated bibliography of completed and ongoing research is intended to assist policymakers, employee benefit specialists, researchers, and others interested in the retirement income field. The entries themselves are arranged alphabetically by title. In the Subject Index (Pt. 6), under "Minorities/Women as Participants in Retirement Income Programs," there are some 85 references to completed or ongoing research on women.

EMPLOYMENT AND EARNINGS, March 1983. Washington, D.C., U.S. Government Printing Office, 1983. 160 pp.

This issue of a monthly report is based, like all the reports, on household interviews and reports from employers, as surveyed each month, and is almost entirely tables, many by age, race, and sex. Table A-3 and A-4 (pp. 31-34) give statistics for women, by age 16-70, of the employment status of the civilian noninstitutional population. Other tables by age/sex include unemployed persons and duration of unemployment (p. 45); employed civilians by class of worker; employed civilians, seasonally adjusted (p. 62); unemployed persons, seasonally adjusted (p. 62).

Estes, Richard J. DIRECTORY OF SOCIAL WELFARE RESEARCH CAPABILITIES: A WORKING GUIDE TO ORGANIZATIONS ENGAGED IN SOCIAL WORK AND SOCIAL WELFARE RESEARCH. Ardmore, Pennsylvania, Dorrance & Co., 1981. 129 pp.

The description of each agency includes the research priorities (as profession focused on fields of practice, special populations, and practice modes.) The number "26" under SPECIAL POPULATIONS indicates that women are a subject of research (age group not indicated) at that agency. One can also use the subject index under Women, and search out the agencies desired.

EVERYWOMAN'S GUIDE TO COLLEGES AND UNIVERSITIES. Ed. by Florence Howe, et al. Old Westbury, New York, Feminist Press, 1982. 512 pp.

This guide is addressed specifically to women. It offers advice and data on American colleges and universities for the young student as well as the older woman considering entry into, or a return to, higher education for her development or employment.

Fallo-Mitchell, Linda and Carol D. Ryff. Preferred Timing of Female Life Events. RESEARCH ON AGING. 4(2):249-267 (June 1982)

This research involved 240 women, in three groups--young, middle-aged, and old. From the results of the Age Constraint Scale administered to all, it was found that the greatest differences were between the young and the old. For example, for family life events, the young preferred later ages than the old preferred. It was observed that for general events the three groups failed to understand each other, and that there are "social clocks" which indicate appropriate times for life cycle events.

Federation of Organizations for Professional Women. WOMEN'S YELLOW PAGES: 570+
ORGANIZATIONS CONCERNED WITH WOMEN'S ISSUES. Washington, D.C., [1981?].
100 pp. Looseleaf.

Lists 570 public and private organizations concerned with women's issues,
including officers, addresses and telephone numbers.

Fengler, Alfred P. and Nicholas Daniels. Residences, the Elderly Widow and Life
Satisfaction. RESEARCH ON AGING. 4(1):113-135 (March 1982)

Fourteen hundred urban and rural disadvantaged widows in northwestern
New England were chosen for research. Limited income and health difficulties were found to be greater disadvantages for the elderly widows
than where they lived (urban or rural). Those living with relatives or
among friendly neighbors found life more satisfactory than living alone.
Includes statistics. Extensive references.

Fengler, Alfred P. and Nancy Goodrich. Wives of Elderly Disabled Men: the
Hidden Patients. GERONTOLOGIST. 19(2):175-183 (April 1979)

Research on disabled older people and their families is just now focusing
on the impact of the illness on the caregiving elderly spouse or family
members, individuals who have special needs and problems if the caregiving
results in low morale.

Ferraro, Kenneth F. and Charles M. Barresi. Impact of Widowhood on the Social
Relations of Older Persons. RESEARCH ON AGING. 4(2):227-247 (June 1982)

This paper compares the situation before widowhood with that after. It
assesses the impact of widowhood on the social relations of the elderly.
The surprise finding was the extent of stability in family relations among
the recently widowed. Social contact with those outside the family tended
to decrease with the years.

Fillmer, H. Thompson. Stereotyping of the Elderly by Children. EDUCATIONAL
GERONTOLOGY. 8(1):77-85 (January/February 1982)

Research indicated that the elderly are stereotyped by all media, but that
young girls and boys have different attitudes toward associating with old
women and men. Their descriptions of old women were more favorable than
those they made of old men. Girls were more willing than boys to associate
with old women. Some data by sex.

Fingerhut, L. Changes in Mortality Among the Elderly: United States, 1940-1978.
VITAL AND HEALTH STATISTICS, SERIES 3, ANALYTIC STUDIES, No. 22, March 1982.
45 pp.

This publication, from the National Center for Health Statistics, gives not
only mortality rates here and abroad, but causes of death and projections
of the growth of the elderly in the future. The importance of the

lessening death rate and the graying of the population as these trends apply to Social Security and labor force participation are also discussed. Fourteen detailed tables are given, most by sex.

Finkelhor, Dorothy C. TRIUMPH OF AGE: HOW TO FEEL YOUNG AND HAPPY IN RETIREMENT. Chicago, Follett Publishing Co., 1979. 264 pp.

This is a "how-to" book, much of it directed to women who have reached an older age and retired. It happily discusses many problems which arise in retirement, including communicating with younger people, how to make critical decisions, sex, making one's marriage better than before, and even offers suggestions for predicting one's future.

Fischer, Lucy Rose. Transition to Grandmotherhood. INTERNATIONAL JOURNAL OF AGING AND HUMAN DEVELOPMENT. 16(1):67-78 (1983)

This exploratory study summarizes previous research on the grandparenting role, both in society and in the family, and notes the confusion in the definition of "grandparent." Forty-three daughters and 39 of their mothers were used to define the ambiguous term "grandmother" based on the interactions between grandmother and grandchild. Discusses the accessibility of the grandmother to the grandchild (i.e. geographical distance and the grandmother-daughter rather than the grandmother-son relationship).

Fisher, Ida and Byron Lane. WIDOW'S GUIDE TO LIFE: HOW TO ADJUST/HOW TO GROW. Englewood Cliffs, New Jersey, Prentice-Hall, Inc., 1981. 207 pp.

Takes the woman from recent widowhood through the legal steps, the accounting and tax problems, her search for stability and on to a new identity. This guide is brief, direct and presented in simple terms, worthy of being consulted and followed.

Foerster, David H. SOCIAL SECURITY: AN NEA POLICY PAPER. Washington, D.C., National Education Association, November 1982. 40 pp.

Recommends steps for strengthening the soundness of the Social Security system. Considers that discrimination against women should be of special concern, and identifies six major areas of discrimination embedded in the law.

Fox, Vivian C. and Martin H. Quitt. LOVING, PARENTING AND DYING: THE FAMILY CYCLE IN ENGLAND AND AMERICA, PAST AND PRESENT. New York, Psychohistory Press, Publishers, 1980. 487 pp.

Two sections on "Spouse Loss" (Introduction, pp. 49-61 and Ch. 6, pp. 400-478) concern family problems caused by the loss of father or mother, particularly the economic situation of the wife with fatherless children. Emphasis is on the wife/widow rather than the husband. The law of England (followed in the American colonies) sustained the status and support of the widow. Contrary to much of the research thus far, widows did not rush into remarriage, and a majority of them were not young people, but rather middle-aged with adult children--especially in the colonies.

Friedman, Joseph and Jane Sjogren. Assets of the Elderly as They Retire. SOCIAL SECURITY BULLETIN. 44(1):16-31 (January 1981)

How personal assets change as older persons approach and enter retirement. Statistics by sex.

Fuller, Marie Marshall and Cora Ann Martin, eds. OLDER WOMEN: LAVENDER ROSE OR GRAY PANTHER. Springfield, Illinois, Charles C. Thomas, 1980. 343 pp.

The editors, in putting together this "anthology," were at first surprised to find so very few studies indicated as being on older women. This surprise was lessened in part, when on examination of the literature, the editors noted that the titles of many articles obscured the fact that older women were indeed being written about, and again when a reading of the articles revealed that in many of them the sex was hidden behind the use of the generic terms, "he" and older "person." The editors suggest that one could almost argue that most of the gerontological literature is about older women, and that older men are the ones really missing. The title of the collection is meant to suggest that older women exhibit greater differences than similarities, hence the aggressive gray panther or the retiring lavender rose. The reprints are all of material from the earlier 1970s, and with the exception of one (a first printing of a 1978 study by Letitia T. Alston and J.P. Alston, "Religion and the Older Woman"), are not abstracted separately in this bibliography. However, the complete contents of the book are as follows:

Williams, Blanch. A Profile of the Elderly Woman. pp. 5-8.
Payne, Barbara and Frank Whittington. Older Women: an Examination of Popular Stereotypes and Research Evidence. pp. 9-30.
On Growing OLder Female: an Interview With Tish Sommers. pp. 31-34.
Beeson, Diane. Women in Studies of Aging: a Critique and Suggestion. pp. 35-44.
Berry, Jane. Do Special Folks Need Special Strokes? Counseling Older Women: a Perspective. pp. 45-49.
Toussie, Carol Grace. Mabel, You Don't Belong Here. pp. 50-52.
Martin, Cora A. Lavender Rose or Gray Panther. pp. 55-58.
Kline, Chrysee. The Socialization Process of Women. pp. 59-70.
A Crabbit Old Woman Wrote This. pp. 71-72.
Baldwin, Faith. My Crabbed Age. pp. 75-78.
Sherr, Virginia T. Benjamin Franklin and Geropsychiatry: Vignettes for the Bicentennial Year. pp. 79-87.
Lobsenz, Norman M. Sex and the Senior Citizen. pp. 88-98.
Graber, Edward A. and Hugh R. K. Barber. The Case for and Against Estrogen Therapy. pp. 99-112.
Stinnett, Nick, Linda M. Carter, and James E. Montgomery. Older Persons' Perceptions of Their Marriages. pp. 113-123.
McKain, Walter C. A New Look at Older Marriages. pp. 124-136.
Fengler, Alfred P. Attitudinal Orientation of Wives Toward Their Husband's Retirement. pp. 137-150.
Wakin, Edward. Living as a Widow: Only the Name's the Same. pp. 151-157.

Johnson, Elizabeth S. and Barbara J. Bursk. Relationships Between
    the Elderly and Their Adult Children. pp. 158-169.
Arling, Greg. The Elderly Widow and Her Family, Neighbors, and
    Friends. pp. 170-189.
Powers, Edward A. and Gordon L. Bultena. Sex Differences in Intimate
    Friendships of Old Age. pp. 190-208.
Mother and Daughter Back in School. pp. 209-210.
Lewis, Myrna I. and Robert N. Butler. Why is Women's Lib Ignoring
    Old Women? pp. 211-222.
Kuhn, Maggie. Grass-Roots Gray Power. pp. 223-227.
Redmond, Rosemary. Legal Issues Involving the Older Woman.
    pp. 228-233.
Bernstein, Merton C. Forecast of Women's Retirement Income: Cloudy
    and Colder; 25 Percent Chance of Poverty. pp. 234-246.
Sommers, Tish. Social Security: a Woman's Viewpoint. pp. 247-261.
Alston, Letitia T. and Jon P. Alston. Religion and the Older Woman.
    pp. 262-278.
Blazer, Dan and Erdman Palmore. Religion and Aging in a Longitudinal
    Panel. pp. 279-285.
Hochschild, Arlie Russell. Communal Life-Styles for the Old.
    pp 289-303.
Lally, Maureen, et al. Older Women in Single Room Occupant (SRO)
    Hotels: A Seattle Profile. pp. 304-316.
Hahn, Aloyse. It's Tough to be Old. pp. 317-319.
Palmore, Erdman. The Future Status of the Aged. pp. 323-331.
Neugarten, Bernice L. The Aged in the Year 2025. pp. 332-343.

Fullerton, Howard N.. and James J. Byrne. Length of Working Life for Men and
    Women, 1970. In: Hendricks, Jon and C. David Hendricks, eds. DIMENSIONS
    OF AGING: READINGS. Cambridge, Massachusetts, Winthrop Publishers, Inc.,
    1979. pp. 309-315.

    In the United States, the average length of an individual's working life
    mirrors changes in longevity, labor force participation, and lifestyle.
    Data from 1970 working life tables indicate that since 1960 worklife
    expectancy has continued to edge downward for men and to lengthen for
    women. These expectancy tables for women are for selected age ranges from
    20 to 65. The striking feature about recent growth in women's worklife
    expectancy is that it has occurred among married women, including those
    with children.

Gelfand, Donald E. AGING: THE ETHNIC FACTOR. Boston, Little, Brown & Co.,
    1982. 113 pp. (Little, Brown Series on Gerontology)

    Continuous statements, separating out the ethnic older woman for specific
    comment, are rare and interspersed. But in a small section on "Ethnic
    Identification" (pp. 91-93), an interesting table is presented on
    "Significance Attached to Various Aspects of Ethnicity by Generation"
    (grandmothers, mothers, daughters).

Gelfand, Donald E. MENTAL HEALTH CONCERNS OF OLDER WOMEN. College Park, Maryland, National Policy Center on Women and Aging, University of Maryland, 1983. 58 pp. (Working Paper 5)

This research is presented under three topics: 1) mental health classifications; 2) prevalence of mental disorders among older women; and 3) mental health policy options. The policy options should ensure that effective treatment meets the needs of older women, with the mental health and aging professionals giving them increased attention and viewing them as a priority population group. Discusses the feasibility of the suggested policy options according to several factors: size of the health unit, personnel attitudes, and funding possible.

George, Linda K. ROLE TRANSITIONS IN LATER LIFE. Monterey, California, Brooks/ Cole Publishing Co., Division of Wadsworth, Inc., 1980. 159 pp. (Brooks/ Cole Series in Social Gerontology)

The early chapters of this book set up a model of the stresses which would be discernible in later life, and the balance of the book applies the stress model to role shifts or patterns. Parenting is a transient pheno-menon, and so is grandparenting, and even adjustment to family alienation. Widowhood is the most dramatic family-based role transition, and is more the problem of women than men, especially for those 65 years of age or older. Even the possibility of remarriage is less for the widow than for the widower. Widows do have access to much family or social support in establishing a new life. The efficacy of the stress model is estimated in Ch. 8 for the many transitions in life. Extensive bibliography: pp. 143-151.

George Washington University. Women's Studies Program and Policy Center. OLDER WOMEN: THE ECONOMICS OF AGING. Washington, D.C., 1980. 57 pp.

In this day-long seminar, public and private specialists considered older women's economic problems and developed policy options for them, suggesting that: data on older women must be improved; the public must be made more aware of women and their heterogeneity; public and private pen-sions must be reformed to provide adequate income; encouragement to employment and more realistic conditions for it must be created; enhanced independence encouraged; and income supplement and design of delivery ser-vice programs improved.

George Washington University. Women's Studies Program and Policy Center. WORKSHOP ON GROWING OLDER FEMALE: THE NEEDS AND RESOURCES OF AGING WOMEN. Washington, D.C., 1980. 6 pp.

This report was presented to the United Nations Mid-Decade Forum, Copenhagen, Denmark, July 13-24, 1980, and gives the results of two three-hour workshops carried out in concert with the recommendation on the sta-tus of older women adopted at the Mexico City Conference. The workshops agreed that women over 65 are usually the poorest of the poor. Among other points, it was agreed that Social Security was inequitable to women (especially divorced older women), that homemakers were discriminated against, and that widowhood was an especially difficult period.

Gerbner, George. WOMEN AND MINORITIES IN TELEVISION DRAMA, 1969-1979. Philadelphia, University of Pennsylvania, Annenberg School of Communication, October 1979. 25 pp.

This study on the representation of women and minorities (defined as non-whites, Hispanics, young and old people) in television casting, has a few direct statements on the older women on prime time television. See Figs. 11, 12, and 13 for statistics on age-role castings of men and women characters representing ages 5-80+ years.

Gesino, Jack Paul, Holly Hamlett Smith and Walter A. Keckich. Battered Woman Grows Old. CLINICAL GERONTOLOGIST. 1(1):59-67 (Fall 1982)

This research is based on two women admitted to the geropsychiatric unit of a hospital for the treatment of depression. These women were not only battered by their husbands, but elected to continue in the same marital relationships regardless. The death or disability of the husband leaves the battered widow with about the same problems as other older widows.

Giambra, Leonard M. Sex Differences in Daydreaming and Related Mental Activity From the Late Teens to the Early Nineties. INTERNATIONAL JOURNAL OF AGING AND HUMAN DEVELOPMENT. 10:1-34 (1979-80)

Using the Imaginal Processes Inventory, Giambra examined aspects of day-dreaming and associated mental activity for sex differences in 1,200 well-educated middle and upper middle-class whites aged 17 to 92 years. Females reported fewer sexual daydreams than males. Most sex differences lasted over the lifetime.

Gibson, Rose Campbell. Race and Sex Differences in Retirement Patterns. NCBA QUARTERLY CONTACT. (National Caucus & Center on Black Aged). 5(2): 7-9 (Summer 1982)

The study centered on older black females who headed families, and examined whether retirement took place early (before age 72); whether the individual remained continuously retired; and what were the major deter-minants of early retirement. Black female heads of families are among the poorest of the poor; such families make up a large segment of the black poor; and there is a growing concern that these women may pass their poverty on to their children. These three characteristics constitute several important reasons for focusing on this segment of the older black woman.

Gibson, Rose Campbell. WORK AND RETIREMENT: AGING BLACK WOMEN: A RACE AND SEX COMPARISON. Ann Arbor, Institute of Gerontology, University of Michigan, December 1982. 112 pp.

This study showed aging black women are less continuously engaged in work than similar white women and fill the lowest level occupations. This discontinuity of work is especially true of black female heads of house-holds. Black female heads of families and widows are particularly in need of counseling on their problems. Many aging black females have no control over their work conditions but do desire full-time employment above their normal low level of occupation. Research is needed to see why these women do not have access to a type of counseling and employment program that would further their ambitions. Similarly, research is needed on why black women retire early--especially significant for Social Security policy. Many tables, most by age and some by sex. Bibliography pp. 109-112.

Giele, Janet Zollinger. Future Research and Policy Questions. In: Giele, Janet Zollinger, ed. WOMEN IN THE MIDDLE YEARS: CURRENT KNOWLEDGE AND DIRECTIONS FOR RESEARCH AND POLICY. New York, John Wiley & Sons, 1982. pp. 199-240.

Giele lists several pressing problems of women in coming decades: 1) How can women gain equal treatment in the labor force? 2) What will happen to children if mothers work? 3) Can men's roles change also? 4) What will become of older women, and how can their lives even now be planned so that they can avoid poverty and isolation? She points out that these current pressing questions were not forseen by the sociological theorists of the 1950s as their model of women's lives at that time was still based on the changes that had accompanied industrialization over a century before. Even World War II did not interrupt that pattern permanently. Giele suggests that the movement of women into the labor force, now in ever growing numbers, calls for recognition of a new model or life pattern accommodating the dual role of women simultaneously in the home and in the work force, and brings up the idea of the crossover between the male and the female roles.

Giele, Janet Zollinger. Women in Adulthood: Unanswered Questions. In: Giele, Janet Zollinger, ed. WOMEN IN THE MIDDLE YEARS: CURRENT KNOWLEDGE AND DIRECTIONS FOR RESEARCH AND POLICY. New York, John Wiley & Sons, 1982. pp. 1-35.

Most earlier research on the adult experience was written by and about men. Giele suggests that mere intellectual thoroughness demands that attention be given to the distinct adult dilemmas and issues experienced by women. Author mentions two apposite points of view: whether any sex differences will be found in the adult development of women and men, or whether any valid theory already encompasses the experience of both sexes. In her opinion, in the end, the actual adult experiences of women and men reveal both similarities and differences. Giele cites the literature already available and makes suggestions as to how future research should be conducted and in what specific areas.

Giele, Janet Zollinger, ed. WOMEN IN THE MIDDLE YEARS: CURRENT KNOWLEDGE AND DIRECTIONS FOR RESEARCH AND POLICY. New York, John Wiley & Sons, 1982. 283 pp. (Wiley Series on Personality Processes)

In 1976, under the sponsorship of the Social Science Research Council, the Study Group on Women was formed. Several meetings showed the necessity of publishing the findings and research discussed at those meetings in book form with chapters on the major dimensions of women's midlife experience: work roles and work histories; psychological issues; health, sexuality and the midlife change, with the theme of needed research and practical programs and policies running throughout. This book is the result. Contents (all articles abstracted separately in this bibliography except the one with asterisk):

Giele, Janet Zollinger. Women in Adulthood: Unanswered Questions. pp. 1-35.
Nathanson, Constance A. and Gerda Lorenz. Women and Health: The Social Dimensions of Biomedical Data. pp. 37-87.
Gilligan, Carol. Adult Development and Women's Development: Arrangements for a Marriage. pp. 89-114.
Giele, Janet Zollinger. Women's Work and Family Roles. pp. 115-150.
* Ecklein, Joan. Women in the German Democratic Republic: Impact of Culture and Social Policy. pp. 151-197.
Giele, Janet Zollinger. Future Research and Policy Questions. pp. 199-240.
Antonucci, Toni C. Longitudinal and Cross-Sectional Data Sources on Women in the Middle Years. pp. 241-274.

Giele, Janet Zollinger. Women's Work and Family Roles. In: Giele, Janet Zollinger, ed. WOMEN IN THE MIDDLE YEARS: CURRENT KNOWLEDGE AND DIRECTIONS FOR RESEARCH AND POLICY. New York, John Wiley & Sons, 1982. pp. 115-150.

In just three decades, the social role of most middle-aged women has changed drastically from the earlier role of marrying right after college, quickly having several children, and giving little thought to needing or wanting a job when they were 45. Today, it is impossible to project any one life-pattern for a given woman, but the challenge to researchers is to understand the reasons for change and also discern the types of life patterns that seem most adaptive under the new social conditions. Giele shows the historical trends in women's social roles since 1950, especially work and family life, and which of the new patterns have been most supportive of women's satisfaction achievement. She discusses the "crossover" in sex roles whereby many tasks are interchangeable; the impact of her family and children on a woman's work pattern; and the reverse, the impact of her work life on her family, children, home life, and housework.

Giesen, Carol Boellhoff and Nancy Datan. The Competent Older Women. In: Datan, Nancy and Nancy Lohman, eds. TRANSITIONS OF AGING. New York, Academic Press, 1980. pp. 57-72.

Aging in general is perceived in a negative manner. Increasing age for women is perceived even more negatively than that for men, a double standard not surprising in a society where such a double standard for the sexes has long been the norm. The authors suggest that this negative attitude is an inaccurate reflection of their actual competence, based on misconceptions: 1) that a woman has never been required to attain a level of competence similiar to that of a man, and 2) that increased age decreases competence in dealing with everyday problems. They suggest furthermore that women have built up competence as they went about their everyday living (if they were not earners outside the home), abilities which they do not suddenly relinquish with older years.

Gilligan, Carol. Adult Development and Women's Development. In: Giele,
    Janet Zollinger, ed. WOMEN IN THE MIDDLE YEARS: CURRENT KNOWLEDGE AND
    DIRECTIONS FOR RESEARCH AND POLICY. New York, John Wiley & Sons, 1982.
    pp. 89-114.

    A number of authors in recent psychological research papers on the midlife
    period of women have suggested developmental schemes that give a time
    sequence and even a chronological age by which a certain stage of develop-
    ment should be attained, as for instance in Erikson's eight stages of man.
    Gilligan questions if this model is truly applicable to women, but does
    not yet propose any grand new theoretical model in its place. She
    discusses women's personality and work in the middle years, and points out
    that the adulthood of women is one of care and responsibility, not care-
    fully enough observed and evaluated to really define the developmental
    psychology of women.

Ginzberg, Eli, et al. WORK DECISIONS IN THE 1980s. Boston, Auburn House
    Publishing Co., 1982. 137 pp.

    Discussion of paid employment in the life of workers. The older worker's
    relation to each phase of employment is given with frequent attention to
    male and female characteristics. See especially Ch. 2, "Economic
    Challenges Posed by Demographic Changes," by Michael E. Borus, and Ch. 4,
    "Postponing Retirement," by Richard P. Nathan, where statistics are given
    by sex.

Glick, Paul C. The Future Marital Status and Living Arrangements of the
    Elderly. GERONTOLOGIST. 19(3):301-309 (June 1979)

    Population projections to the year 2000 and a discussion of the marital
    status and living arrangements of elders (men and women) at that time.
    Tables by age/sex.

Golding, N.G. Family and the Older Adult. In: Harris, Charles S., ed.
    CHANGING LANDSCAPE: SOCIAL, ECONOMIC, AND POLITICAL TRENDS IN AMERICA
    AND THEIR IMPLICATIONS FOR OLDER AMERICANS. Washington, D.C., National
    Council on the Aging, Inc., 1980. pp. 25-77.

    This is one of four monographs prepared by the National Council on the
    Aging in anticipation of the 1981 White House Conference on Aging, the
    four of them addressing major institutions of American society: the
    family, the community, economic institutions, and political institutions.
    The mission of this monograph was to provide, in this case, basic infor-
    mation on family trends and the older adult. It is the one most concerned
    with the older woman, and almost every page takes note of her problems and
    status: employment; spouse caring; post parenthood; widowhood; divorce;
    economics; loneliness; and family relationships. Monograph concludes
    with policy suggestions in areas of: employment; housing of the older
    widowed, divorced or single person; voluntarism; support systems;
    counseling; financial assistance; and abuse of the elder person, some of
    which policies would directly affect a woman.

Gonzalez Del Valle, Amalia and Mary Usher. Group Therapy with the Aged Latino
Women: A Pilot Project and Study. CLINICAL GERONTOLOGIST. 1(1):51-58
(Fall 1982)

Report of a pilot project offering mental health counseling to elderly
Latino women. The experiment in group therapy was declared a success, but
it was also predicted that, with pre-group interviews and a clear understanding of the achievements to be expected from the therapy, many
pitfalls of this pilot group could be avoided.

Gordon, Nancy M. Institutional Responses: the Social Security System. In:
Smith, Ralph E., ed. SUBTLE REVOLUTION: WOMEN AT WORK. Washington,
D.C., Urban Institute, 1979. pp. 223-254.

Changing social and demographic trends have major importance for the
Social Security system, especially with respect to the older woman. The
relative treatment of one-earner couples, two-earner couples, and single
individuals must be addressed, as well as the inadequacy of old-age income
protection for divorced homemakers. This article focuses on the retirement and aged-survivors portions of the Social Security system. It examines
first the provisions of the current system and their undesirable consequences for certain groups (again, women especially), and then describes
the proposed policy alternatives and their underlying rationales.
Concludes with future costs of such options.

Grad, Susan. INCOME OF THE POPULATION 55 AND OVER, 1978. Washington, D.C.,
U.S. Government Printing Office, December 1981. 74 pp. (U.S. Social
Security Administration. Office of Research & Statistics, SSA Pub. 13-
11865, 1978)

Among the 74 tables presented on the income of the elderly 55 and over,
17 are presented by age/sex, including persons not yet retired, partly
retired, and fully retired. The aged without Social Security benefits are
a small minority, as most persons 65+ are Social Security beneficiaries.
Blacks are among the poorest since they are less likely to derive income
from any pension other than Social Security.

Grady, Sally C. MENTAL HEALTH AND AGING: AN IN-SERVICE TRAINING GUIDE.
Lansing, Michigan, Office of Services to the Aging, March 1982. 106 pp.

Provides information and resources in the form of in-service training
guide to be used as a tool for people in human service agencies interested
in the mental health problems of older adults. The chapters on
"Widowhood," "Retirement," and "Physical and Health Changes in Aging"
especially touch on women's problems. Bibliography pp. 101-106. "Basic
Library," pp. 3-6.

Graney, Marshall J. and Doris M. Cottam. Labor Force Nonparticipation of Older
People: United States, 1890-1970. GERONTOLOGIST. 21(2):138-141 (April
1981)

Analysis of U.S. census data, 1890 to 1970, provides reasons for the
decreased labor force participation of older men and women.

Gratton, Brian and Marie R. Haug. Decision and Adaptation: Research on
Female Retirement. RESEARCH ON AGING. 5(1):59-76 (March 1983)

Review of the literature shows that while women's adaptation to retirement
has been closely studied, little is known of their decisions to retire.
This literature review notes the factors in the timing of the decision
to retire (including sex differences, marital status, spouse influence)
and also the nature of a woman's adjustment to retirement (noting that
she adjusts more successfully than earlier studies suggested). Since the
retirement of women is the emerging problem in the older labor force,
research on their reasons for retirement has implications for Social
Security among other areas.

Gratton, Brian. Labor Markets and Old Ladies' Homes. In: Markson, Elizabeth
W., ed. OLDER WOMEN: ISSUES AND PROSPECTS. Lexington, Massachusetts,
Lexington Books, D.C. Heath & Co., 1983. pp. 121-149.

Examines the earlier work pursuits of elderly women who had worked outside
the home and then spent their last years in the Boston House for Aged
Women (HAW), a charity that sheltered the housekeepers, laundresses, nurse-
maids, and "ethnic sisters" of the Brahmins of Boston, founded 1849 precisely for "women who had the misfortune to have to work in a time when
proper women did not have to." An examination of the institutional archives
of this home reveals the development of philanthropy for the aged and
the potential and limitations of such charity. The HAW was at once
liberated by its sympathy for the dependent older women and hampered by
ethnic and class biases. It was the first charity for the aged (in this
case for aged women) established by a compact group of elite reformers
seeking to create a new look at welfare in antebellum Boston. They set up
the rigorous frame within which 19th century urban charity was to be
dispensed, with regulations and points of view which persisted for many
years in the United States.

Haber, Carole. BEYOND SIXTY-FIVE: THE DILEMMA OF OLD AGE IN AMERICA'S PAST.
Cambridge, England, Cambridge University Press, 1983. 181 pp.

This is a scholarly discussion of the causes and conditions of old age
throughout the earlier history of America. Because there is so little
written in this period, the two chapters in this book which differentiate
the two sexes in some of the discussion are welcome. Chapter 1, "Aging in
Colonial America," gives a general picture of the wife and widow. Chapter
5, "Institutionalizing the Elderly," is interesting for the description of
the early almshouses and poorhouses, the earlier ones being dedicated to
the indigent single woman and the widow. Such refuges for men came later.

Hand, Jennifer. Shopping-Bag Women: Aging Deviants in the City. In: Markson, Elizabeth W., ed. OLDER WOMEN: ISSUES AND PROSPECTS. Lexington, Massachussetts, Lexington Books, D.C. Heath & Co., 1983. pp. 155-177.

Shopping-bag women are women who, finding themselves continuously alone, socially unattached, and homeless, walk out into the street with their possessions in containers ranging from paper bags to small carts, and make a place for themselves there. Hand estimates that in New York City, in 1976, between 400 and 600 such women had fended for themselves for at least a year. Despite their situation, they uncover resources and make a claim to space, property, and independence, even as they avoid institutional controls. Homeless people find it difficult to maintain self-respect and social status as against their needs for social support. Maintaining a solitary state is one defense. The author made this 1976 survey of shopping-bag women in the Greenwich Village area of Manhattan. She describes how she found them, their characteristics (including "aloneness"), how they made a living and where they sheltered themselves in the changing seasons.

Harrill, Inez, Mary Kunz and Anne Kylen. Dietary Supplementation and Nutritional Status of Elderly Women. JOURNAL OF NUTRITION FOR THE ELDERLY. 1(3/4):3-13 (Fall/Winter 1981)

A balanced, that is nutritionally-sound, supplement to the food of elderly women can be helpful to general well-being. A dietary supplement is not equally useful to all elderly, and should not be administered without physician approval.

Harrill, Inez and Mildred M. Bowski. Relationship of Age and Sex to Nutrient Supplement Usage in a Group of Adults in Colorado. JOURNAL OF NUTRITION FOR THE ELDERLY. 1(3/4):51-64 (Fall/Winter 1981)

This was an investigation of the extent to which nutritive supplements were used by older people and by younger people. Seventy-five percent of all the respondents used nutritive supplements, most prevalently among young women. Older women were more apt to use the supplement to prevent colds.

Harris, Louis, & Associates, Inc. AGING IN THE EIGHTIES: AMERICA IN TRANSITION: A SURVEY CONDUCTED FOR THE NATIONAL COUNCIL ON THE AGING, INC. Washington, D.C., National Council on the Aging, November 1981. 169 pp.

This is a followup to its 1975 survey, MYTH AND REALITY OF AGING IN AMERICA. The study makes clear the tangible progress being made by older people, and puts into focus the continuing vulnerability of the lower income aged, older women, minority aged and the old-old. Throughout the numerous tables, the data are differentiated by sex in areas such as work and retirement, economics, and emerging issues.

Hartz, Arthur J. and Alfred A. Rimm. Natural History of Obesity in 6,946 Women Between 50 and 59 Years of Age. AMERICAN JOURNAL OF PUBLIC HEALTH. 70(4):384-388 (April 1980)

In reconstructing the weight history of this group of women from about age 20 on, the author found that the majority were not obese by age 20. Of those 100% overweight in their 50s, 16% were not obese at any time during their first 30 years. The history of obesity prior to age 30 was not associated with weight gain between ages 30 and 50, suggesting there is no critical time for development of obesity, and that previous weight history is not a dominant factor in determining subsequent weight gain. This is an interesting study in view of the fact that few studies have investigated the development of obesity during adulthood.

Heisel, Marsel A., Gordon G. Darkenwald and Richard E. Anderson. Participation in Organized Educational Activities Among Adults Age 60 and Over. EDUCATIONAL GERONTOLOGY. 6(2/3):227-240 (March/April 1981)

Results of a study in which a national data base was used for the first time to examine in detail the educational participation behavior of adults over 60. Women were 66% of those surveyed. Several paragraphs and two tables address themselves to women: what subjects do they study (Table 2, p. 233) and why do they seek adult education (Table 4, p. 236). In the conclusion and discussion, women again are addressed.

Heisel, Marsel A. and Audrey O. Faulkner. Religiosity in an Older Black Population. GERONTOLOGIST. 22(4):354-358 (August 1982)

Study of religion in the lives of aging poor urban blacks. Ninety-three women and 29 men were studied. Sex did not show a relationship to church membership, but age did. Also, women alone seemed to turn to the church for social activity. Authors point out that this is a study of one area, and they do not wish to generalize from it. Some statistics by sex.

Helsing, Knud J., Moyses Szklo and George W. Comstock. Factors Associated with Mortality After Widowhood. AMERICAN JOURNAL OF PUBLIC HEALTH. 71(8):802-809 (August 1981)

Study in a semi-rural area of Maryland of 2828 females and 1204 males (white and over 18) who became widowed between 1963 and 1974 and of an equal and matched number of married persons. The purpose was to see what the death rate of widowed women and men was in comparison to still married women and married men.

Hendricks, Jon and C. Davis Hendricks. AGING IN MASS SOCIETY: MYTHS AND REALITIES. 2d ed. Cambridge, Massachusetts, Winthrop Publishers, Inc., 1977. 304 pp.

An examination of the table of contents of Hendricks' second edition does not suggest the number of statements actually included on women. Every several pages, they refer to age/sex statistics; the impact of the growing population of women (and hence older women) on our daily lives; women's special problems; and the inequalities of even the norms of treatment in society. Chapter 2 presents historical data of life expectancy of women in various areas, 1-400 A.D. (see p. 65); percentage by sex of individuals dying between 50-70 years of age in European ruling classes in the 16th-19th centuries; life expectancy of women in the Plymouth Colony; life expectancy at age 20 for European aristocratic females between 1550-1909. Chapter 3, "Aging in Advanced Industrialized Societies," presents general population trends with some statistics. Chapter 10, "Family Life and Living Arrangements," treats the trauma of separation and widowhood. In short, the relationship of the older woman to the totality of the social and economic life is not disregarded in this treatment of aging in mass society.

Henretta, John C. and Angela O'Rand. Labor-Force Participation of Older Married Women. SOCIAL SECURITY BULLETIN. 43(8):10-16 (August 1980)

Analyzes why working wives stop working, based on the 1969, 1971, and 1973 waves of the Longitudinal Retirement History Study. Younger wives were more apt to work than older wives. Among working wives, what determines the timing of the reduction of work when approaching old age is addressed in this article. Although the patterns were somewhat different for young wives, both the coverage of the wife by a private pension plan and the need to provide support for children or elderly parents have substantial effects on the probability of continuing to work.

Herzog, Anna Regula. Attitude Change in Older Age: an Experimental Study. JOURNAL OF GERONTOLOGY. 34(5):697-703 (September 1979)

The role of age in the attitude change process was experimentally studied by exposing older and younger women to persuasive information, presented at different speeds. In general, the higher speed levels which were employed to decrease information reception resulted in less attitude change, but no overall age differences in the amount of attitude change were observed.

Hess, Beth B. and Joan Waring. Family Relationships of Older Women: a Women's Issue. In: Markson, Elizabeth W., ed. OLDER WOMEN: ISSUES AND PROSPECTS. Lexington, Massachusetts, Lexington Books, D.C. Heath & Co., 1983. pp. 227-251.

Authors examine the potential dimensions and familial sources of old-age dependency among women. The care of an aged frail husband falls quite often on the spouse. But in the case of the aged frail wife (or widow), the care in old age falls on the children, most often on the daughter. With the emergence of working women who now frequently work into their own late middle age, the care of the aged parent constitutes a double role for the caregiver. The authors fear that the current trend in public policy seeks to curtail Federal support for programs assisting the elderly: entitlements to income; housing; transportation; and health care. Hess and Waring place the needs of female caregivers and caretakers high up on the list of necessary public policy. Six pages of references appended.

Hess, Beth B. Old Women: Problems, Potential, and Policy Implications. In: Markson, Elizabeth W. and Gretchen R. Batra, eds. PUBLIC POLICIES FOR AN AGING POPULATION. Lexington, Massachusetts, Lexington Books, D.C. Heath and Co., 1980. pp. 38-59.

Future policy for older women should be influenced by their uncertain income resources as well as by their longer life expectancy over men and their greater proportion in the population to the end of the century. Their growing proportion in the labor force and their improved health status are additional influences in policy consideration.

Hess, Beth B. Sex Roles, Friendship, and the Life Course. RESEARCH ON AGING. 1(4):494-515 (December 1979)

In the past sociologists have been principally concerned with behaviors of men rather than women. Males and females differ greatly in friendship behaviors. The author in this article concentrates on friendship and the interaction of sex and age with it.

Hing, Esther and Beulah K. Cypress. Use of Health Services by Women 65 Years of Age and Over. VITAL & HEALTH STATISTICS, SER. 13, DATA FROM THE NATIONAL HEALTH SURVEY, No. 59, August 1981. 72 pp.

Examines health care resource utilization by elderly women beginning with ambulatory care in physicians' offices through hospital care to nursing home care, and points to the general course of treatment sought by the older woman. The pattern of a hospital stay followed by a stay in a nursing home applies more often to elderly women than to elderly men (post-hospital care in the home appears to be more available to elderly men because they are more likely to have a spouse at home).

Hoffman, Adeline M. CLOTHING FOR THE HANDICAPPED, THE AGED, AND OTHER PEOPLE WITH SPECIAL NEEDS. Springfield, Illinois, Charles C. Thomas, 1979. 192 pp.

Information on the provision of clothing for people with special needs, emphasizing the physically handicapped, the aged, the chronically ill and the mentally retarded. Attention to female needs highlighted.

Hoffman, Ellen. FEDERAL ROLE IN LIFELONG LEARNING. New York, College Entrance Examination Board, 1980. 32 pp.

Discusses policy for young and old. However, 26 million women (displaced homemakers, single mothers, and the elderly) are identified as having special urgent and unmet educational needs. Policy recommendations are included.

Holden, Karen C. The Inequitable Distribution of OASI Benefits Among
    Homemakers. GERONTOLOGIST. 19(3):250-256 (June 1979)

    Argues that spouse benefits create disparities among women in the Old Age
    and Survivors Insurance benefits they receive for periods of not working, and
    that the disparities are inconsistent both with the insurance and with the
    income transfer features of the program.

Holden, Karen C. Public Pensions for Nonworking Wives: Policy Choice and Equity
    Questions. RESEARCH ON AGING. 1(1):65-82 (March 1979)

    Examines how completely nonworking women are protected against income loss
    in old age by OASI (Old Age and Survivors Insurance program) and makes a com-
    parison with similar protection in Japan.

Holden, Karen C. Spouse and Survivor Benefits: Distribution Among Aged Women.
    RESEARCH ON AGING. 1(3):301-318 (September 1979)

    Examines the income redistribution effects of the additional benefits
    available to wives and widows above those for which they are eligible as
    retired workers. The results show that additional benefits paid to wives
    do not target aged poor couples and cannot be justified on antipoverty
    grounds.

Hollenshead, Carol and Berit Ingersoll. Middle-Aged and Older Women in Print
    Advertisements. EDUCATIONAL GERONTOLOGY. 8(1):25-41 (January/February
    1982)

    Study examined images of aging women as depicted in advertisements from
    three periodicals during a ten-year period. Five variables were
    considered: frequency of appearance, types of products involved, the
    setting, the value orientation, and the change in the image of older women
    over the ten years.

Holt, Margaret E. Myth Understanding for Mid-Life Women. LIFELONG LEARNING.
    6(3):20-21;30 (November 1982)

    Although adult educators have not neglected the intellectual needs of mid-
    life women, there is still much research needed to identify, to
    understand, to make widely known, and thereafter to meet their special
    needs. These women often require special training as they decide to
    "launch out" on their own.

Hooyman, Nancy R. Mutual Help Organizations for Rural Older Women. EDUCATIONAL
    GERONTOLOGY. 4(5):429-447 (October/December 1980)

    The author points out that rural older women are more numerous than men,
    more likely to be widowed or single, and are more prone to the usual risks
    which accompany later life. There is very little major research specifi-
    cally on the rural older woman. The author suggests that mutual help
    organizations would meet some of their needs.

Horvath, Francis W. Job Tenure of Workers in January 1981. MONTHLY LABOR
    REVIEW. 105(9):34-36 (September 1982)

    Close to 30% of all workers during January 1981 had been on their jobs
    less than one year. However, nearly one-fourth had been at the job more
    than 10 years. Overall, the median job tenure was 3.2 years. In this
    report, three of the tables are presented by age/sex.

Humphrey, John A., R. Page Hudson and Steven Cosgrove. Women Who Are Murdered:
    an Analysis of 912 Consecutive Victims. OMEGA. 12(3):281-288 (1981-1982)

    A study of all female homicide victims in North Carolina, 1972 through
    1976. In the "Findings" (pp. 283-284), authors give statistics on the homi-
    cides by sex/age and cite an increase among elderly white females of about
    26% in that period. Thus, despite a decrease in general of homicides,
    formerly low risk groups (older persons, male and female) have emerged as
    increasingly vulnerable to homicidal death.

Hyman, Herbert H. OF TIME AND WIDOWHOOD: NATIONWIDE STUDIES OF ENDURING
    EFFECTS. Durham, North Carolina, Duke University Press, 1983. 118 pp.
    (Duke Press Policy Studies)

    This book is a study of what widowhood does, short term and long term,
    to the white woman involved. It is based on longitudinal and cross-
    sectional analyses of 650 widows in comparison with 2,000 married women in
    the mid-20th century. Conclusions are stated to be "tentative," and
    additional studies are urged. There is also a small study of similar
    problems among widowed men.

International Conference of Social Gerontology, 9th, Quebec, August 27-28, 1980.
    ADAPTABILITY AND AGING. Paris, International Center of Social
    Gerontology, May 1981. 2 vols. (333 + 494 pp.)

    These two volumes constitute a pioneering effort on the part of international
    specialists to provide information on aging and adaptability as background
    material for the 1982 World Assembly on Aging. In the first section of
    Vol. 2 (pp. 9-100) of these proceedings, "Women and Aging," several
    articles address themselves to the American woman (abstracted separately
    in this bibliography):

        Shock, Nathan. Biological and Physiological Characteristics of
            Aging in Men and Women. pp. 9-27.
        Brickfield, C.F. Women in Their Later Years: a Time of New
            Challenges. pp. 43-48.
        Kuhn, Margaret E. Changing the Status and Role of Older Women.
            pp. 59-64.
        Lesnoff-Caravaglia, G. Aging of Women: a Biological Betrayal.
            pp. 85-88.

Jackson, Jacqueline Johnson. MINORITIES AND AGING. Belmont, California,
     Wadsworth Publishing Co., a Division of Wadsworth, Inc., 1980. 256 pp.

     In this work on aging among adult minorities and associated problems and
     issues, Jackson gives due attention to the women in these minority groups,
     but includes Anglo-American women in the statements and tables in order to
     extend the descriptive information and comparison. The minorities studied
     (in detail or briefly) are: American Indians, Chinese Americans, Japanese
     Americans, Filipino Americans, Korean Americans, Hawaiian Americans, and
     black Americans. Three chapters are of special concern to this
     bibliography. Chapter 2 is on "Demographic Aspects of Minority Aging."
     The 9 statistical tables go back to 1900 or to 1930. Chapter 4 is on
     "Mortality and Life Expectancy Patterns of Aging Minorities," and the 7
     tables here again present data by sex/race (black, non-white and white,
     the latter again for comparison). Four of the 7 tables are for causes
     of death (diseases, accidents, homicide, suicide). Chapter 6 is on
     "Social Aspects of Minority Aging" (marital status, living arrangements,
     employment, and voting patterns). All 8 tables are by age/sex. Jackson
     strongly recommends more rigorous and sophisticated research, including
     mixtures of cross-sectional and longitudinal studies of representative
     samples of various age cohorts over time, again reminding us that major
     demographic trends point to the ever-increasing female proportion in the
     number of aged persons living alone. A selected bibliography on pp. 227-
     249.

Jacobs, Ruth Harriet. LIFE AFTER YOUTH: FEMALE, FORTY--WHAT NEXT? Boston,
     Beacon Press, 1979. 168 pp.

     Assessment of the older woman's social role in America and suggestions
     for breaking through the restrictive roles women now play and for
     broadening the options open to older women.

Jacobs, Ruth Harriet. Out of the Mikvah, Into the Sauna: a Study of Women's
     Health Clubs. In: Markson, Elizabeth W., ed. OLDER WOMEN: ISSUES AND
     PROSPECTS. Lexington, Massachusetts, Lexington Books, D.C. Heath & Co.,
     1983. pp. 49-54.

     Author examined the health club and the type of women who frequented seven
     such New York City clubs. Many of these women had a decade earlier been
     involved in similar groups, the health club being the current favorite.
     These clubs provided socialization which did not extend outside the club
     to "displaced" women (divorced, widowed and the older never married) and
     a health regime to those genuinely interested in that aspect. The re-
     stricted social role of many older women makes the health club attractive,
     although participation in the club may narrow the individual's participa-
     tion in a wider social life.

Jaslow, Philip. Employment, Retirement, and Morale Among Older Women. In:
     Hendricks, Jon and C. David Hendricks, eds. DIMENSIONS OF AGING: READINGS.
     Cambridge, Massachusetts, Winthrop Publishers, Inc., 1979. pp. 315-331.

     While numerous studies have been reported on the relationship between
     labor force participation and social-psychological well-being among older
     men, only speculation has prevailed on this subject regarding elderly

women. The analysis revealed that employed women normally had higher morale than retirees (some exceptions among retirees who had enjoyed the higher salaries). Women who had never worked were found to have the lowest morale as a group. The analysis here reported involved 2,398 women, and variables measured included: morale, general health, physical incapacity, employment, age and income.

Jennings, Jerry T. Social and Economic Characteristics of Americans During Midlife. CURRENT POPULATION REPORTS. SERIES P-23 (SPECIAL STUDIES), No. 111, 1981. 54 pp.

This report consolidates data on the social and economic characteristics of the middle-aged population between 45 and 64 years old, much of it by sex. Among the characteristics presented in graphic form are family and marital status, fertility, mobility, residence, educational attainment, voting, labor force participation, occupation and industry, income and earnings, poverty status, health, and crime victimization.

Jewson, Ruth Hathaway. After Retirement: an Exploratory Study of the Professional Woman. In: Szinovacz, Maximiliane, ed. WOMEN'S RETIREMENT: POLICY IMPLICATIONS OF RECENT RESEARCH. Beverly Hills, California, Sage Publications, 1982. pp. 169-182.

An exploration of what retirement is like for professional women in their first six years of retirement based on a non-random sampling of 162 members or former members of the National Council on Family Relations. The findings showed the retirees had positive feelings about their retirement. All were relatively healthy and financially independent, and the author wonders if changed health and less financial independence ten years from then might not alter their feelings about retirement at that later date. This group found satisfaction in its ability to identify and use a wide variety of options: enter into new careers, enjoy friendship networks and family, use leisure time profitably, and savor financial security. The author suggests preretirement counseling and education be offered in the workplace, schools, churches, and community agencies well before retirement age.

Johnson, Elizabeth S. Older Mothers' Perceptions of Their Child's Divorce. GERONTOLOGIST. 21(4):395-401 (August 1981)

The experiences of 250 older women and of their friends, with a divorced child: traumatic, painful, and sad.

Johnson, Elizabeth S. Role Expectations and Role Realities of Older Italian Mothers and Their daughters. INTERNATONAL JOURNAL OF AGING AND HUMAN DEVELOPMENT. 14(4):271-276 (1981-1982)

Reports role responsibilities of Italo-American mothers and daughters to each other. At least 75% of both agreed they should each offer advice, emotional support and general availability, including assistance on finances and chores. Adult daughters felt the need for advice or emotional support less than the mothers.

Johnson, Elizabeth S. Suburban Older Women. In: Markson, Elizabeth W., ed.
    OLDER WOMEN: ISSUES AND PROSPECTS. Lexington, Massachusetts, Lexington
    Books, D.C. Heath & Co., 1983. pp. 179-193.

    Johnson notes that, in sharp contrast to urban shopping-bag women, there
    are equally diverse older women who have "grayed" within their suburban
    setting. They continue to inhabit the same suburb (some without spouses
    or children, or ties to particular agencies or institutions). The author
    interviewed 39 women, 65 years of age or older, residents of a small com-
    munity on the edge of a larger center, who discussed their personal
    histories and past and present relationships with others, disclosing
    their satisfactions or dissatisfactions (many of these related to children
    rather than to place of residence).

Johnston, Denis F. and Sally L. Hoover. Social Indicators of Aging. In:
    Riley, Matilda White, et al., eds. AGING FROM BIRTH TO DEATH, Vol. 2,
    SOCIOTEMPORAL PERSPECTIVES. Boulder, Colorado, Westview Press, Inc.,
    1982. pp. 197-215.

    Authors report on differences between aging men and women with respect
    to perception of the quality of life, pointing out such factors as living
    arrangements, health, education, length of life, income, and labor force
    participation.

Kahana, Boaz and Eva Kahana. Clinical Issues at Middle Age and Late Life.
    In: Berardo, Felix M., ed. Middle and Late Life Transitions. ANNALS
    OF THE AMERICAN ACADEMY OF POLITICAL AND SOCIAL SCIENCE, Vol. 464,
    November 1982. pp. 140-161.

    Mental health problems of middle and late life are the focus of this
    article. Sex differences in adjusting to increased stress during mid-
    life and later years are presented. Since the vast majority of the very
    old are women who are increasingly outliving men, special attention must
    be paid to mental health problems unique to elderly women: 1) poverty,
    2) widowed status, and 3) social isolation. Contrary to long-held
    beliefs, women in mid-life are not necessarily susceptible to menopause-
    associated depression. Authors discuss other stress-related sources of
    depression.

Kahana, Eva F. and H. Asuman Kiyak. The Older Woman: Impact of Widowhood and
    Living Arrangements on Service Needs. JOURNAL OF GERONTOLOGICAL SOCIAL
    WORK. 3(2):17-29 (Winter 1980)

    Interviews were conducted with 302 older persons to determine their
    problems and needs for community services. Older women who had never
    married required fewer social services than older widows.

Kahne, Hilda. ECONOMIC SECURITY OF OLDER WOMEN: TOO LITTLE FOR LATE IN LIFE.
    Waltham, Massachusetts, Florence Heller Graduate School, Brandeis
    University, June 1981. 47 + 9 pp. (Brandeis University, National
    Aging Policy Center on Income Maintenance Monographs, No. 1)

Facts on the increasing proportion of women over age 65, who are usually poorer than men of the same age. This poverty seems likely to increase also as most public and private retirement systems do not take into account that women's work is intermittent and much of it at home. Kahne proposes immediate and long-term improvements, especially in Social Security, for women's economic security. Bibliography (9 pp.) at end.

Kahne, Hilda. Women and Social Security: Social Policy Adjusts to Social Change. INTERNATIONAL JOURNAL OF AGING AND HUMAN DEVELOPMENT. 13(3): 195-208 (1981)

Discusses the lack of congruence between the Social Security program's provisions for women and their contemporary social roles.

Kannel, William B. and Frederick N. Brand. Cardiovascular Risk Factors in the Elderly Woman. In: Markson, Elizabeth W., ed. OLDER WOMEN: ISSUES AND PROSPECTS. Lexington, Massachusetts, Lexington Books, D.C. Heath & Co., 1983. pp. 315-327.

In 1975, in the United States, among people 65 and over, there were 69 men for every 100 women. This sex ratio reflects the male versus the female mortality at each age level. Sex differences in mortality are due principally to differential rates of coronary heart disease, in which women fare definitely better than men. While heart disease is still the leading cause of death in the U.S., the rate has declined (more for women than men) considerably in the last 24 years, proving that it is a preventable disease. However, hypertension, greater for women then men after age 44, is cause for concern because of its relationship to heart disease and strokes. The discussion on hypertension and coronary heart disease in this article is based on the Framingham Epidemiological Heart Disease Study begun in 1949 to trace these diseases.

Karp, David A. and William C. Yoels. EXPERIENCING THE LIFE CYCLE: A SOCIAL PSYCHOLOGY OF AGING. Springfield, Illinois, Charles C. Thomas, 1982. 208 pp.

The authors state their aim is to deal with the subjective, personal responses that persons make to aging in the course of their lives and not to treat the aged as a group by themselves. The chapter, "Men, Women, and Life-Cycles," stresses sex roles. Subsections on "Widowhood" and "Response to Retirement" are particularly valuable to understanding older women.

Kasworm, Carol and Janice Wood Wetzel. Women and Retirement: Evolving Issues for Future Research and Education Intervention. EDUCATIONAL GERONTOLOGY. 7(4):299-314 (December 1981)

This article examines the current status of research regarding women and retirement and discusses the multiple issues that surround the aging woman and her relationship to the retirement process. Suggests future preretirement educational programming.

Keith, Pat M. Life Changes and Perceptions of Life and Death Among Older Men and Women. JOURNAL OF GERONTOLOGY. 34(6):870-878 (November 1979)

Study examines whether life changes are associated with concurrent life and death attitudes among older men (214) and women (354).

Keith, Pat M. Life Changes, Leisure Activities, and Well-Being Among Very Old Men and Women. ACTIVITIES, ADAPTATION AND AGING. 1(1):67-75 (Fall 1980)

Life changes may precipitate a social breakdown syndrome among the aged whereby persons tend to accept a label as incompetent and see themselves as sick or inadequate. Involvement in leisure activities may interrupt the cycle and initiate a change in attitude. Data from interviews with 214 men and 354 women, 72 years of age or older are analyzed. Leisure involvement, it was found, is somewhat sex-linked, and participation influences the well-being of men and women in different ways.

Keith, Pat M. Sex Differences in Household Involvement of the Unmarried. JOURNAL OF GERONTOLOGICAL SOCIAL WORK. 2(4):331-343 (Summer 1980)

Discusses sex differences in the management of household tasks by the unmarried, sources of help they secure, and the relationship among psychological well-being, personal characteristics, and involvement in household tasks.

Keith, Pat M. Working Women Versus Homemakers: Retirement Resources and Correlates of Well-Being. In: Szinovacz, Maximiliane, ed. WOMEN'S RETIREMENT: POLICY IMPLICATIONS OF RECENT RESEARCH. Beverly Hills, California, Sage Publications, 1982. pp. 77-91.

Heretofore, comparison of elderly retired women has usually been made with retired men, not with elderly homemakers. This is an analysis of the personal and social resources of these two groups of women and how these resources influence their psychological well-being in very old age. The author suggests that in the future employment may make more difference in women's sense of well-being than what this research indicated, as women become more committed to non-traditional occupations.

Keller, James F. and George A. Hughston. COUNSELING THE ELDERLY: A SYSTEMS APPROACH. New York, Harper & Row Publishers, 1981. 168 pp.

This book represents an attempt at incorporating the numerous strategies for psychological intervention with older persons, and comments that such an approach presupposes an understanding of demographic trends and physiological developments in the aging years. Many techniques are presented with model case study examples, some of men, some of women. Ch. 1, "Trends and Numbers," gives tables and statements by sex on: population statistics; life span; and characteristics by sex as to income, race, marital status, family status, labor force participation, and living arrangements. Bibliography: pp. 157-163.

Kerzner, Lawrence J. Physical Changes After Menopause. In: Markson, Elizabeth W., ed. OLDER WOMEN: ISSUES AND PROSPECTS. Lexington, Massachusetts, Lexington Books, D.C. Heath & Co., 1983. pp. 299-313.

Discusses some of the physical and physiological changes that occur with aging in women, including pre-menopause; cardiovascular disease; falls and fractures; and osteoporosis. Use of estrogens in treatment is discussed at some length.

Kestenbaum, Bert and Greg Diez. Mortality of Older Widows and Wives. SOCIAL SECURITY BULLETIN. 45(10):24-26 (October 1982)

This research (1973-1980) was undertaken to discover if there are any mortality differences between widows and wives, 60 years of age and over, who receive Social Security benefits, and other widows and wives, 60 years or over, who do not receive Social Security benefits. Authors also sought to find out if length of widowhood makes any difference in mortality. The findings are displayed in tables that, contrary to the original hypotheses of the study, show the mortality rates of the Social Security Administration records are no higher (even lower) than those from the vital statistics system.

King, Nancy R. and Marjory G. Marvel. ISSUES, POLICIES AND PROGRAMS FOR MIDLIFE AND OLDER WOMEN. Washington, D.C., Center for Women Policy Studies, 1982. 166 pp.

The changing trend from previous minimal research on the older woman to a current increasing interest in her status and issues led the Center for Women Policy Studies to conduct a survey of organizations and programs throughout the United States to determine the level of involvement in issues and activities relevant to women over 45. Of the 300 organizations contacted, 24 had programs of national significance which are described in this report (Section 3, pp. 102-132). Section 1 of the text provides an overview of the status of midlife and older women and the major issues and policies which affect them. This information is used to evaluate the current level of programmatic development and assess future needs. This first section is supported by statistical information and includes a substantial bibliography of the literature cited. Section 2 gives a brief history and description of the programmatic and policy developments which benefit midlife and older women (including Federal policies and programs affecting the aging). Section 4 is a list of selected resources by program (pp. 146-156) and by subject area (pp. 157-166). This publication is basic reading for those interested in issues, policies and programs for the mature woman.

King, Nancy R. Sexuality, Sex Differences and Age. In: OCCASIONAL PAPERS IN MENTAL HEALTH AND AGING. Salt Lake City, University of Utah, Gerontology Program, 1981. pp. 129-152.

The author cites six myths concerning old age and then refutes them completely or at least reduces their significance. She finds differences between aging men and aging women. Quoting such authorities as Kinsey, Masters and Johnson, or the Duke Study, she notes, for example, that women are "sexually more stable," "less inhibited" with the years. King also reports on the effect on sexuality in women of illness, drugs, and nutrition. In conclusion, she adds some observations of her own, declares the need for future research, and finally suggests how practitioners, even with our present limited knowledge, can meet the needs of older people-- especially older women.

Kirk, Cynthia Formanek and Lorraine T. Dorfman. Satisfaction and Role Strain Among Middle-Age and Older Reentry Women Students. EDUCATIONAL GERONTOLOGY. 9(1):15-29 (January-February 1983)

The major purposes of this study were to investigate a broad range of variables associated with satisfaction and strain experienced in the student role by mature reentry women students and to develop and test a model for predicting satisfaction and role strain in these students. Extensive references.

Kivett, Vira R. Religious Motivation in Middle Age: Correlates and Implications. JOURNAL OF GERONTOLOGY. 34(1):106-115 (January 1979)

Study of 301 men and women, aged 45 to 65, to determine the relative relationship of religious motivation in middle age to self-rated health, age, sex, race, self-concept, education, occupation and locus of control. Women were less likely than men to show a self-centered dependence on religion.

Kivnick, Helen Q. Grandparenthood and the Mental Health of Grandparents. AGEING AND SOCIETY. 1(3):365-391 (November 1981)

What it means to older men and women to be grandparents, the role of grandparenthood through the individual life cycle and the relationship between grandparenthood "meaning" and mental health.

Kivnick, Helen Q. MEANING OF GRANDPARENTHOOD. Ann Arbor, Michigan, UMI Research Press, 1982. 236 pp. (Research in Clinical Psychology, No. 3)

Study of the meanings that grandparenthood seems to hold for most grandparents; the connections among the recalled experience as a grandchild, expectations of being a grandparent, and actual experiences; and the connections between grandparenthood and mental health. The sample of population in the survey consisted of 212 grandmothers and 74 grandparents, one-third of them under 65 years of age. Table 2 presents, by percentage and sex, the variables (age, marital status, education, work status, housing, health, income, number of grand-, great-grand and great-great-grandchildren, and religion). Grandmotherhood is separately treated in two sections: grandmotherhood and grandchildhood (pp. 108-116); and grandmotherhood: procedures and findings (pp. 123-127), both with tables. Author finds that grandparents have various and different kinds of thoughts about their role, one being that it takes on different kinds of meaning and importance to her/him, and helps to counteract some measure of the decrease in morale which often accompanies growing old.

Kroeger, Naomi. Preretirement Preparation: Sex Differences in Access, Sources, and Use. In: Szinovacz, Maximiliane, ed. WOMEN'S RETIREMENT: POLICY IMPLICATIONS OF RECENT RESEARCH. Beverly Hills, California, Sage Publications, 1982. pp. 95-111.

Compares preretirement preparation efforts made by a sample of workers (264, mostly non-executives) recently retired from the retail trade (both those who had participated in formal programs or who had worked out their own "self-help" programs) with retirees who reported that they had not made any effort to anticipate the difference in life-style after retirement. Men were more likely to use informal sources, whereas women relied somewhat more on formal programs where they were available, but in general were much more likely to have had no retirement preparation at all. The conclusion is that more of the formal type of information and programs should be available to the women planning to retire.

Kruzas, Anthony T., ed. SOCIAL SERVICE ORGANIZATIONS AND AGENCIES DIRECTORY. Detroit, Michigan, Gale Research Co., 1982. 525 pp.

This reference guide to national and regional social service organizations, Section 45, pp. 430-457, lists women's organizations and includes many devoted to the older woman, or whose general interests would encompass the older woman. Information includes address, personnel and program. State and Federal government agencies listed with addresses and phone numbers.

Kubelka, Susanna. OVER FORTY AT LAST. New York, Macmillan Publishing Co., Inc., 1982. 237 pp.

The author proclaims this "an exuberant book." She expresses delight that she has arrived at an age of discernment, judgment, and confidence. She has no fear of later age, and recommends to other women her experience and enthusiasm. This book is a translation of her 1980 German edition, "Endlich Ueber Viersig."

Kuhn, Margaret E. Changing the Status and Role of Older Women. In: International Conference of Social Gerontology, 9th, Quebec, August 27-28, 1980. ADAPTABILITY AND AGING, Vol. 2. Paris, International Center of Social Gerontology, May 1981. pp. 59-64.

Author discusses the economic and social causes of poverty among aging women, who the older they grow, the poorer they become, suggesting older women live in "quadruple" jeopardy: outliving men, they exist on diminishing resources; they have low income in their working years; they are lonely survivors in their old age; and their medical problems are underestimated and neglected. Author mentions role of the Gray Panthers in meeting the needs of older women.

Lake, Alice. OUR OWN YEARS: WHAT WOMEN OVER 35 SHOULD KNOW ABOUT THEMSELVES.
New York, A Woman's Day/Random House Book, 1979. 243 pp.

The psychological, social and physical problems and issues that face
women at midlife, including: years of freedom, menopause, sex, the
woman's heart, cancer, middle-age spread, changes in skin and hair, the
back and the bones; eyes and teeth; memory and stress; and concluding with
a look at the future.

Lally, Maureen, et al. Older Women in Single Room Occupant (SRO) Hotels: a
Seattle Profile. GERONTOLOGIST. 19(1):67-73 (February 1979)

Life histories and daily routines of 16 women over age 55 living in 10
Seattle single room occupancy hotels were studied, using both observations
and interviews. The purpose of the study was to obtain information on the
backgrounds of these women, how they became inner-city residents, and how
they manage their lives and cope with their environments. The authors
found that these hotel residents placed a premium on their independence,
but that the lifestyle precluded easy access to social services which they
needed from time to time, or at a crisis, especially in the area of
health. Lally, et al., suggest an informal network of contacts which would
link the hotel residents with these social services.

Lapkoff, Shelley. WORKING WOMEN, MARRIAGE, AND RETIREMENT. Washington, D.C.,
President's Commission on Pension Policy, August 1980. 50 pp.

Society has changed a great deal from the time when Social Security was
set up to provide income maintenance for the family of the bread-winning
husband. Three of the most significant changes have been the increased
participation of women in the labor market, rising divorce rates, and the
increased longevity of women relative to men. The majority of women over
65 now are without spouses and constitute a very large proportion of the
elderly poor. The changes in family roles and marital status affect the
retirement income of women who have earlier worked or are now widows and
divorcees. The first section of the paper treats Social Security and
problem areas for women. The second section is on employee pension plans
and is speculative and exploratory.

LaRue, Asenath, et al. Health in Old Age: How Do Physicians' Ratings and
Self-Ratings Compare? JOURNAL OF GERONTOLOGY. 34(5):687-691 (September
1979)

Study examined the relationship between self-reports of health and
physicians' ratings. The sample of aged people consisted of 69 survivors
of an initial sample of 268 aged twins who had been studied longitudinally,
beginning in 1947 to 1949. At the time of the health assessment the survivors ranged in age from 77 to 93. Findings suggested that self-ratings
are a useful index of health in old age. The results are cited by sex in
the text as well as in three tables.

Lee, Gary R. Sex Differences in Fear of Crime Among Older People. RESEARCH
ON AGING. 4(3):284-298 (September 1982)

Previous research had supported the idea that women aged 55+ are more
fearful of crime than men, but differed in that women were fearful of specific types of crime. This research checked 2262 elderly women for their
reaction to 13 different possible criminal acts, finding that walking alone
at night in certain areas was their greatest fear. It is also reported
that sex differences in all other respects are negligible.

Leonard, Frances, Virginia Dean, Alice Sharp and Margaret Malberti. THE
DISILLUSIONMENT OF DIVORCE FOR OLDER WOMEN. Washington, D.C., Older
Women's League, August 1980. 20 pp. (Gray Paper, No. 6)

Authors point out that the no-fault divorce acts have too often proved
disastrous to older women who in their mid-to-older years find themselves
in a changed marital state, the shocks of which are not cushioned by
social support systems, income maintenance guarantees, nor enlightened property concepts. As women become "unemployed" as wives and are forced to
find other jobs, they encounter multiple obstacles: they are inexperienced
and there is a dearth of the kinds of work mostly filled by women and
especially by older women. This Gray Paper focuses on those aspects of
divorce which affect the midlife to older woman who has devoted much or
all of her married life to homemaking alone or homemaking in combination
with a "non-career" job: 1) impact of no-fault divorce detrimental to the
dependent homemaker; 2) support and property needs; 3) victimization of
the newly divorced older woman; 4) handling of the divorce process; and
5) strategies for minimizing the consequences of divorce for the older
woman.

Leonard, Frances, Tish Sommers and Virginia Dean. NOT EVEN FOR DOGCATCHER:
EMPLOYMENT DISCRIMINATION AND OLDER WOMEN. Washington, D.C., Older
Women's League, December 1982. 23 pp. (Gray Paper, No. 8)

The authors call attention to the double burden of ageism and sexism which
the older woman encounters in seeking entry to the paid labor force, and
note that the legal remedies of recent years intended to widen opportunities for minorities, women, and older workers do not necessarily
accomplish those goals with the older woman. The older woman fares badly
as against the more attractive young woman. In comparison to the older
man seeking entry or re-entry to the work force, she presents herself as
inexperienced, whereas the older man presents a work experience history.
The discrimination occurs in the wage scale, which is not necessarily
determined by equal qualification and production. The signs of discrimination are difficult to detect, even by the victim herself, or she
unconsciously has come to accept discrimination on the job, notwithstanding the intent of the Age Discrimination in Employment Act. The authors
suggest strategies for reform or enforcement of existing legislation.

Lesnoff-Caravaglia, Gari. Aging of Women: a Biological Betrayal. In:
International Conference of Social Gerontology, 9th, Quebec, August 27-28,
1980. ADAPTABILITY AND AGING, Vol. 2. Paris, International Center of
Social Gerontology, May 1981. pp. 85-88.

The author reminds us that, of the life changes to which older women are
subject, the growing realization by a woman that she has passed from being
a "nurturer" (mother, teacher, nurse, and homemaker) to the post-
menopausal state in which she feels "superfluous" constitutes the dominant
change in the aging process for which she must develop her own individual
coping methods. The author discusses the special needs of American women
in meeting these problems.

Lesnoff-Caravaglia, Gari. The Black "Granny" and the Soviet "Babushka":
Commonalities and Contrasts. In: Manuel, Ron C., ed. MINORITY AGING.
Westport, Connecticut, Greenwood Press, 1982. pp. 109-114.

The black older woman in America, like the "babushka" in Russia, has
traditionally filled society's need for a granny to assist the survival of
generations, reassuming the childcaring role for grandchildren and even
unrelated children. She may even continue to work and take on this care
simultaneously. One study noted that two thirds of black children under
age 18 and living with relatives are grandchildren of the head of the
household. Because of economic pressures, the black granny often was
regarded as the economic mainstay, and the focal point in the family
assistance scheme. She shares with her dependent family whatever
"largess" comes to her. Although evidence points to extensive relations
between black females and the grandchildren, it is also true that a
greater percentage of the black aged (relative to white aged) do not
have grandchildren.

Levy, Sandra M. The Adjustment of the Older Woman: Effects of Chronic Ill
Health and Attitudes Toward Retirement. INTERNATIONAL JOURNAL OF AGING
AND HUMAN DEVELOPMENT. 12(2):93-110 (1980-1981)

In this survey of 52 female retirees, it was found that both healthy and
ill females who had not initially wanted to retire did not adjust over
time to the retirement state. In addition, it was found that chronically
ill females were not uniform in terms of maladjustment, that a significant
portion of ill female interviewees was seemingly able to surmount the
effects of bodily disease and adjust to the transition to retirement.

Liang, Jersey. Sex Differences in Life Satisfaction Among the Elderly.
JOURNAL OF GERONTOLOGY. 37(1):100-108 (January 1982)

This research could find no consistent main effects of sex on morale or
its determinants. The research was carefully done by sex, and conclusions are contrary to those reached by earlier researchers. Tables by
sex.

Lingg, Barbara A. Social Security Benefits of Female Retired Workers and Two-
    Worker Couples. SOCIAL SECURITY BULLETIN. 45(2):3-24 (February 1982)

    Presents the 1976 situation of the never-married and other single
    (divorced, widowed) retired workers, but concentrates on the income bene-
    fits and entitlements of the women partners of married couples. The
    single retired female worker, based on her own earnings, benefits most,
    the white more than the black female. Statistics by sex, race and age.

Lingg, Barbara A. Women Social Security Beneficiaries Aged 62 and Older, 1960-
    1979. SOCIAL SECURITY BULLETIN. 43(7):28-31 (July 1980)

    In 1930, 24% of all women worked, then comprising 22% of the total work
    force. In 1979, 51% of all women worked and represented 41% of the total
    work force. This has changed the benefits on retirement which they and
    their children receive from Social Security.

Livson, Florine B. Patterns of Personality Development in Middle-Aged Women:
    a Longitudinal Study. In: Hendricks, Jon, ed. BEING AND BECOMING OLD.
    Farmingdale, New York, Baywood Publishing Co., Inc., 1980. (Perspectives
    on Aging and Human Development Series, Vol. 1) pp. 133-140.

    Livson takes a longitudinal look at personality development from ado-
    lescence to middle age in 24 women who had achieved a relatively high
    level of psychological health by age 50, with special attention to
    changes in the middle adult years (age 40 to 50, a decade which embraces a
    critical transition in the life span). The author suggests that the key
    factor in psychological health is the harmony between a woman's life style
    and her personality, that personality characteristics persist through life
    in most persons.

Loewinsohn, Ruth Jean. SURVIVAL HANDBOOK FOR WIDOWS (AND FOR RELATIVES AND
    FRIENDS WHO WANT TO UNDERSTAND). Chicago, Follett Publishing Co., 1979.
    141 pp.

    The widow is often overlooked and frequently not well understood. The
    years succeeding the loss of a spouse see the widow going through many
    transitions, grieving, silence in loss, sorting of details and daily
    living, possibility of new associations, finally arriving at a new, whole
    personality. This slim volume takes the widow through it all, step by
    step and very practically.

Longino, Charles F., Jr. and Aaron Lipman. The Married, the Formerly Married
    and the Never Married: Support System Differentials of Older Women in
    Planned Retirement Communities. INTERNATIONAL JOURNAL OF AGING AND HUMAN
    DEVELOPMENT. 15(4):285-297 (1982-1983)

    This paper explores the nature of informal support given to older women,
    depending upon their marital status and the presence of living children.
    Extensive references.

Lopata, Helena Znaniecka and Kathleen Fordham Norr. Changing Commitments of American Women to Work and Family Roles. SOCIAL SECURITY BULLETIN. 43(6):3-14 (June 1980)

This research involves 996 Chicago-area women, black and white, aged 25-54, as family members and in employment. Although 58% of these women were employed outside the home, indicating an opening up of many previously closed work areas, the traditional family roles of women persisted.

Lopata, Helena Znaniecka. Economic Support of Women and Children. In: Kolker, Aliza and Paul I. Ahmed, eds. AGING. New York, Elsevier Biomedical, 1982. (Coping with Medical Issues Series) pp. 101-118.

This paper focuses on the economic dependency and poverty of older wives and widows deprived of the husband breadwinner, women who, additionally, had never been breadwinners themselves. Idealization of economic success has prevented society, even that of today, from handling the problems of economic poverty among these women without the breadwinning male. A judgmental character bias attaches itself to much of the public welfare aid for them. This is an interesting historical sketch of the status of the older wife and widow. 58 references.

Lopata, Helena Znaniecka. Meaning of Friendship in Widowhood. In: Steinberg, Laurence D., ed. THE LIFE CYCLE: READINGS IN HUMAN DEVELOPMENT. New York, Columbia University Press, 1981. pp. 368-379.

Lopata gives a short resume of the literature on friendships of the married woman as she is influenced by the marital state; her husband's job requirements; the moving from one geographical area to another; the frequent social disapproval of same-sex friendships or of opposite-sex friendships (either of which may reflect on the idea of the perfect husband-wife companionship). Thus, while friendship is idealized in literature, it may be viewed with caution in real life. She points out that, notwithstanding, there is one group in our society which is encouraged to develop friendships: older people, those persons freed from many of the earlier restraints precisely at an age when new friendships are more difficult to develop. Lopata discusses the meanings and significance of friendships among widows, showing that a surprising number of them are socially isolated, an isolation that is especially true among the lesser educated and the more economically disadvantaged.

Lopata, Helena Znaniecka. The Widowed Family Member. In: Datan, Nancy and Nancy Lohman, eds. TRANSITIONS OF AGING. New York, Academic Press, 1980. pp. 93-118.

Three characteristics of the role complexes, support systems, and life styles of widows and widowers were examined: the similarities and differences in how the manner of death of the spouse and succeeding events affect men versus women; the great heterogeneity of the widowed population; and the emergence of a new type of widow. This "new" widow is able to reconstruct her own self and her support systems to ensure greater "social life space" and independent life style.

Lopata, Helena Znaniecka. Widowhood: Societal Factors in Life-Span Disruptions and Alternatives. In: Schaie, K. Warner and James Geiwitz, eds. READINGS IN ADULT DEVEOPMENT AND AGING. Boston, Little, Brown and Co., 1982. pp. 192-200.

This article focuses on the impact of the death of a spouse (a member of a social unit) on the remaining female spouse in terms such as financial and emotional stability, and role in modern societies.

Lopata, Helena Znaniecka. WOMEN AS WIDOWS: SUPPORT SYSTEMS. New York, Elsevier, 1979. 485 pp.

Based on a study of over 1,000 Chicago area widows, this study provides an historical, descriptive, and theoretical study on widowhood, focusing on the societal, community and personal resources formerly and now available to each widow and how the utilization of these resources builds economic, service, social, and emotional support systems and networks. Survey questionnaire: pp. 391-463. Bibliography pp. 465-777.

Lowenthal, Marjorie Fiske, Majda Thurnher and David Chiriboga. FOUR STAGES OF LIFE. San Francisco, Jossey-Bass Publishers, 1975. 292 pp.

Lowenthal's book is interestingly subtitled: A Comparative Study of Men and Women Facing Transitions. The four stages of life, for what seems to be mainstream America, are primarily job- and family-oriented, and include middle-aged parents and persons about to retire. This is a sociopsychological study whose findings should aid further research on adult life and on catastrophic changes such as divorce or widowhood. Comparison is constantly made between men and women; indeed, sex is said to account for most variations observed. For example, middle-aged men had a positive self-image; women of similar age, a more negative one, whereas preretired women showed characteristics usually attributed to men. This 1975 imprint is included in this bibliography because of its outstanding significance. Bibliography: pp. 263-281.

Lyons, Walter. Coping With Cognitive Impairment: Some Family Dynamics and Helping Roles. JOURNAL OF GERONTOLOGICAL SOCIAL WORK. 4(3/4):3-20 (Spring/Summer 1982)

The author focuses on coping with cognitive impairment at any age, but speaks specifically of his wife, a sufferer of Alzheimer's disease (60% of those suffering from cognitive impairment have Alzheimer's disease). He speaks in detail of the support given the victim by family and social workers.

McGuire, Francis A. Leisure Time, Activities, and Meanings: a Comparison of Men and Women in Late Life. In: Osgood, Nancy M., ed. LIFE AFTER WORK: RETIREMENT, LEISURE, RECREATION, AND THE ELDERLY. New York, Praeger, 1982. pp. 132-147.

This literature review (30 publications and articles are cited) examined three areas: 1) the differing perceptions of older men and women relative to the amount of unobligated time they have; 2) the differential activity involvement of older males and females; and 3) the differences in the meaning of leisure involvement to men and women in their later years. The most marked differences were in activity involvement.

Madden, Myron C. and Mary Ben Madden. FOR GRANDPARENTS: WONDERS AND WORRIES. Philadelphia, Westminster Press, 1980. 118 pp.

Grandparenting has value for the individual, young and old. Grandmothers' lifestyles involve problems, but these are outweighed by the loving, caring relationships established for a lifetime.

Malvestuto, P. and A.J. Svacha. Obesity and Health in the Elderly. JOURNAL OF NUTRITION FOR THE ELDERLY. 1(1):91-100 (Spring 1980)

Subject of this article is the frequency of obesity in age and sex groups and the relationship of obesity to social and physical well-being. In the Alabama study of 169 bi-racial participants, 38% of the women and 9% of the men were obese. Table by sex.

Melatesta, Victor J. The Urban Widow: a Focus for Gerontological Study: the Present Adaptive Status of Two Elderly Urban Widows. In: Montgomery, James E. and Lynda H. Walters, eds. PRESENTATIONS ON AGING. Athens, Faculty of Gerontology/Gerontology Center, University of Georgia, 1980. pp. 9-21.

Author compares the 1975 figures on widows and widowers, 6.2 million of the former, 1.5 million of the latter, and suggests that, even with such numbers and proportions, there is a lack of information and statistics. He stresses that the basis of research on the older widow should begin with a better understanding of widows as individuals and herewith presents two case studies, highlighting problems and types of needed intervention.

Markson, Elizabeth W., ed. OLDER WOMEN: ISSUES AND PROSPECTS. Lexington, Massachusetts, Lexington Books, D.C. Heath & Co., 1983. 351 pp.

Fifteen original articles by different authors on the social diversity of growing old as a woman, reporting on the needs of the growing numbers of older women in our population and the necessity to consider proposals for proper solution to the needs. These problems are examined in four sections: 1) changing bodies, changing selves; 2) older women in the labor market; 3) without and within the family; and 4) health issues in later life. The editor notes that, while women have been the subject of much scholarly and popular attention within the last decade, only recently has research focused specifically on older women and the ways in which their aging processes may be similar or distinct from those of men, ironic in view of their proportional representation in the population. Most of the articles begin with a review of the published literature on the particular subject, sometimes sparse, sometimes generous. In all, the book constitutes not only a subject resource, but also a bibliographic resource on the older woman. Contents (all articles abstracted separately in this bibliography):

Berkun, Cleo S. Changing Appearance for Women in the Middle Years of Life: Trauma? pp. 11-35.

Gognalons-Nicolet, Maryvonne. The Crossroads of Menopause: a Chance and a Risk for the Aging Process of Women. pp. 37-48.

Jacobs, Ruth Harriet. Out of the Mikvah into the Sauna: a Study of Women's Health Clubs. pp. 49-54.

Turner, Barbara F. and Catherine Adams. The Sexuality of Older Women. pp. 55-72.

Rosen, Ellen. Beyond the Sweatshop: Older Women in Blue-Collar Jobs. pp. 75-91.

Szinovacz, Maximiliane E. Beyond the Hearth: Older Women and Retirement. pp. 93-120.

Gratton, Brian. Labor Markets and Old Ladies' Homes. pp. 121-149.

Hand, Jennifer. Shopping-Bag Women: Aging Deviants in the City. pp. 155-177.

Johnson, Elizabeth S. Suburban Older Women. pp. 179-193.

Braito, Rita and Donna Anderson. The Ever-Single Elderly Woman. pp. 195-225.

Hess, Beth B. and Joan Waring. Family Relationships of Older Women: a Women's Issue. pp. 227-251.

Marshall, Victor W., Carolyn J. Rosenthal, and Jane Synge. Concerns about Parental Health. pp. 253-273.

O'Laughlin, Kay. The Final Challenge: Facing Death. pp. 275-296.

Kerzner, Lawrence J. Physical Changes after Menopause. pp. 299-313.

Kannel, William B. and Frederick N. Brand. Cardiovascular Risk Factors in the Elderly Woman. pp. 315-327.

Marshall, Victor W., Carolyn J. Rosenthal and Jane Synge. Concerns About Parental Health. In: Markson, Elizabeth W., ed. OLDER WOMEN: ISSUES AND PROSPECTS. Lexington, Massachusetts, Lexington Books, D.C. Heath & Co., 1983. pp. 253-273.

This article focuses on the need for assistance from adult children and the awareness of such need by the children in protracted health care situations of parents. As women typically outlive their husbands, it is the aged widow/parent who may need to call on adult children for her care. The authors, in their survey of 506 adult children (with 263 parents involved), were interested in the concerns of the adult-child generation in this caregiving situation.

Martin, Cora A. and Susan Brown Eve. CHANGING USE OF HEALTH CARE SERVICES BY UNMARRIED OLDER WOMEN, 1969 TO 1975: FINAL REPORT TO THE NRTA-AARP ANDRUS FOUNDATION. Denton, North Texas State University, Department of Sociology and Anthropology, Center for Studies in Aging, March 1982. 100 pp.

"Major purpose of the research was to examine changes in the use of health care services as older women reach their retirement years, and involved secondary analysis of data on 1,954 older women interviewed in the Social Security Administration Longitudinal Retirement History Study in 1969, 1971, 1973, 1975." The use of physician and hospital services increased from the pre-retirement to the retirement years, and a decreased percentage put off needed health care services during the same period.

Additionally, use of physicians' services was due primarily to the real need for them, i.e., older women who are the least healthy are the most likely to use those services. Again, the older women with the greater financial resources were more likely to utilize the physicians' services, even though their need was proportionately lesser. Hospital insurance coverage, however, leads to increased use of hospital services. In short, the older woman with less economic/income resources is less likely to avail herself of needed health care. Suggestions for policy makers also included.

Masnick, George and Mary Jo Bane. THE NATION'S FAMILIES: 1960-1990. Boston, Auburn House Publishing Co., 1980. 175 pp.

The authors base the information in this study on a cohort analysis of life-course patterns of generations, and describe the changing American family and the implications of these changes for the social and economic future. Ch. 2, "Population, Households, and Families," describes the current trend away from the traditional family structure, and statistical projections to 1990. Ch. 3, "Women's Work and Family Income," gives a picture of present and future female labor force participation; the permanency and continuity of woman's participation; and her contribution to the "family" income. They suggest that by 1990, there is not much reason to expect that the substantial income differences between types of households will change much, as women's earnings as a percentage of men's are increasing only slowly, if at all. Ch. 4, "Changing Families, Changing Times," describes the newer living arrangements and their social and economic impacts. Twenty-seven out of 63 detailed tables are by sex/age, and 12 of the 28 charts, likewise, by sex/age. The statistical information in this book is abundant.

Mathews, Virginia. LIBRARIES: AIDS TO LIFE SATISFACTION FOR OLDER WOMEN: A 1981 WHITE HOUSE CONFERENCE ON AGING BACKGROUND PAPER. Washington, D.C., September 1981. 94 pp.

There is evidence that a large number of older women are not ill nor mentally handicapped, but rather well, alert, seeking new experiences, even paid employment. They vary greatly in their characteristics, including their educational levels. Libraries, particularly in association with other community services such as senior centers, have an opportunity to meet the needs and interests of these women. Illustrations of what these women might do are a substantial part of this pamphlet.

Matthews, Joseph L. and Dorothy Matthews Berman. SOURCEBOOK FOR OLDER AMERICANS. Berkeley, California, Nolo Press, 1983. 279 pp.

Printed in large type, written in easily understood conversational style, this SOURCEBOOK addresses itself principally to Social Security benefits, what they are and how to obtain them; to Medicare coverage; Medicaid; private health insurance; Supplemental Security Income; government, railroad workers and veterans benefits; private pensions; and workings of the Federal Age Discrimination in Employment Act. Where these benefits for women differ from the benefits in general, such differences and applications are clearly stated.

Matthews, Sarah H. SOCIAL WORLD OF OLD WOMEN: MANAGEMENT OF SELF-IDENTITY.
Preface by John Lofland. Beverly Hills, California, Sage Publications,
1979. 192 pp. (Sage Library of Social Research, Vol. 78)

Research on the problems and means of self-protection of women in the
social scene (the social structure) as they grow older physically. One
chapter is devoted to each of the four situations calling for
self-protection: 1) the person stigmatized as an "old" woman; 2) old
widows; 3) old mothers; and 4) women facing death. Two appendices contain
interviewers' guides.

Meier, Elizabeth and Cynthia C. Dittmar. INCOME OF THE RETIRED: LEVELS AND
SOURCES. [Washington, D.C. U.S. Government Printing Office?], October
1980. 87 pp. On cover: Working Papers, President's Commission on Pension
Policy.

Expansion in coverage of public and private retirement systems and
increases in benefit levels have increased the benefits of aged people
drawing retirement income from these sources and produced a dramatic
decrease in poverty rates among those 65 and over. But today's retirement
income programs and individual sources of income still leave millions at
or near the poverty level: 38% of married couples age 65 and over are
still below the 1978 Bureau of Standards intermediate retired couples
budget of $7,486. Throughout the six chapters of this study, statements
and tables illustrate the position of women in this retirement income picture, with respect to the kind and amount, role of savings and earnings,
and retirement income goals.

Meier, Elizabeth. New ERISA Agency Considered and Pension Issues of Women and
Minorities. AGING AND WORK. 3(2):135-137. (Spring 1980)

Women and minorities have problems which arise because they "fall between
the cracks" of pension coverage and receipt. This subject was considered
at the daylong meeting of the President's Commission on Pension Policy.
Another topic treated was society's failure to recognize the value of
women in the home, making the private pension system "anti-homemaker."

Miller, Donald B. CAREERS '80/'81: A HUMAN RESOURCE CONSULTANT'S VIEWS OF
CAREER MANAGEMENT AND DEVELOPMENT AND A GUIDE TO 600 CURRENT BOOKS AND
ARTICLES. 2d ed. Saratoga, California, Vitality Associates, 1980.
267 pp.

This is an up-to-date introduction to career/life planning and management
and is for any adult including older women, who may be engaged in self-
assessment and planning for future life activity. It has special rele-
vance to women, older and younger, as it identifies "family careers."
Furthermore, the index has seven major topics headed "Women" with a
total of at least a hundred specialized references for women such as
"career growth" and "education."

Mindel, Charles H. and Roosevelt Wright, Jr. Use of Social Services by Black and White Elderly: The Role of Social Support Systems. JOURNAL OF GERONTOLOGICAL SOCIAL WORK. 4(3/4):107-125 (Spring/Summer 1982)

The research sample had more females than males. The study points out that "need-for-care" and race were more important in utilization of social services than other factors, especially for the female rural black elderly.

Moss, Miriam S. and Sidney Z. Moss. Image of the Deceased Spouse in Remarriage of Elderly Widow(er)s. JOURNAL OF GERONTOLOGICAL SOCIAL WORK. 3(2):59-70 (Winter 1980)

The remarriage of elders, male and female, their ties to the deceased spouse, the factors encouraging and inhibiting remarriage and the role of the deceased spouse in the new marital relationship.

Mueller, Jean E. Bibliography of Doctoral Dissertations on Aging from American Institutions of Higher Learning, 1979-1981. JOURNAL OF GERONTOLOGY. 37(4):496-512 (July 1982)

This is an ongoing, annual, listing of dissertations in aging, beginning with the first listing (1934-1969) in Vol. 26, No. 3, July 1961, pp. 291-422. This feature generally appears in the July issue of the Journal. In recent years, women as an identifiable subject of research number between 50 and 60 dissertations in each listing as it is issued. Each covers an overlapping period of two years, but with no duplication of titles. The dissertations are in classed arrangement by subject.

Muller, Charlotte F. Economic Roles and the Status of the Elderly. In: Borgatta, Edgar and Neil G. McCluskey, eds. AGING AND SOCIETY: CURRENT RESEARCH AND POLICY PERSPECTIVES. Beverly Hills, California, Sage Publications, 1980. pp. 17-41.

The article contains statements and statistics on the economic roles and the status of the elderly, Social Security, pensions, and income from employment, differentiated by sex.

Nathanson, Constance A. and Gerda Lorenz. Women and Health: the Social Dimensions of Biomedical Data. In: Giele, Janet Zollinger, ed. WOMEN IN THE MIDDLE YEARS: CURRENT KNOWLEDGE AND DIRECTIONS FOR RESEARCH AND POLICY. New York, John Wiley & Sons, 1982. pp. 37-87.

This article attempts to present and evaluate the most recent evidence regarding women's health and physical status with respect to their biological functions and capacities. The authors report a generally positive relationship between employment and health status among women, but a mortality rather higher than expected among certain groups of professional women. The evidence of higher mortality in this group is not sufficiently clear or consistent enough to suggest how future changes in women's occupational status will affect their mortality risks (including suicide rates). Bibliography (13 pp.) appended.

National Council on the Aging, Inc. FACT BOOK ON AGING. Washington, D.C.,
1978. 263 pp.

Facts on aging are presented in eight chapters: Demography; Income;
Employment; Physical Health; Mental Health; Housing; Transportation; and
Criminal Victimization. Text is accompanied by tables and graphs. Under
Demography, there are five tables (out of 10) which present the data by
age/sex. Under Income, only two out of 11; Employment, two out of five;
Physical Health, six out of 16; Mental Health, one out of four; Transpor-
tation and Criminal Victimization, none.

National Council on the Aging, Inc. Public Policy Agenda. PERSPECTIVE ON
AGING. 9(4):12-39 (July/August 1980)

In general, these policy statements consider the needs of elderly women
and elderly men as common to both, without sex distinction. However, in
addressing retirement income, the Council makes note of the poverty of
older women and minorities. In the section on social services, the
Council recommends that the Older Americans Act mandate addressed to
older persons with the greatest economic or social needs, should be
enforced vigorously, and that the needs of low-income, isolated old-old
population (all of which groups consist disproportionately of older women)
should be addressed. In the area of transportation, again, the Council
points out the greater immobility of older women as compared to that of
men.

National Retired Teachers Association/American Association of Retired Persons.
LEARNING ABOUT AGING. Chicago, American Library Association, 1981. 64 pp.

An annotated bibliography designed to help educators introduce the topic of
"aging" to school students and to aid in locating material for curriculum
development and classroom use. One hundred and twenty books and 33 audio-
visual items are cited with suggestions for application. In the subject
index, citations are found under "Older Woman" and "Widowhood."

Neolker, Linda S. and Zev Harel. Residential Choice and the Well-Being of
Aged and Disabled Public Housing Residents. JOURNAL OF GERONTOLOGICAL
SOCIAL WORK. 4(2):17-30 (Winter 1981)

Analysis of the residential preferences of 325 aged females and 102 males,
excluding the disabled. One table, pp. 22-23, gives sociodemographic and
health characteristics of the sample by sex.

Nestel, Gilbert, Jacqueline Mercier and Lois B. Shaw. Economic Consequences of
Midlife Change in Marital Status. In: Shaw, Lois B., ed. UNPLANNED
CAREERS: THE WORKING LIVES OF MIDDLE-AGED WOMEN. Lexington, Massachusetts,
Lexington Books, 1982. pp. 109-125.

After the loss of a spouse, when a woman becomes head of a family in
midlife, she normally increases her labor force participation. Remarriage
seems less likely if the woman is economically well off and well educated.

Older women and black women are less likely to remarry in any case. Research shows that many older women family heads now receive AFDC (Aid to Families with Dependent Children) until the children leave home, followed by 10-25 years of reduced income and diminishing opportunity to work, a situation which continues right through to the retirement age. Poverty is a concomitant characteristic of this group.

New York (City). Department for the Aging. OLDER WOMEN IN THE CITY. New York, Arno Press, a New York Times Co., 1979. 188 pp.

Papers presented at a conference, jointly sponsored by the Commission on the Status of Women and the Department for the Aging, May 1978, at which four major problem areas were treated: emotional and physical health; family and living arrangements; income and finance; and meaningful roles for older women. In her introductory remarks, Alice M. Brophy called attention to the special impact of inadequate income on the older women, not only those who have been poor all their lives, but those newly poor on becoming old. She pointed out that income in old age is especially influenced by the previous work life or marital status.

New York (State). Office for the Aging. FAMILY CAREGIVING AND THE ELDERLY: POLICY RECOMMENDATIONS AND RESEARCH FINDINGS. Albany, March 1983. 71 pp.

In this survey of caregiving arrangements of the family for the elderly, the Beth Soldo study, "Family Caregiving to the Elderly: Prevalence and Variations" (published by the Kennedy Institute, Georgetown University, Washington, D.C., 1980) is cited as finding that these caregivers are predominantly female (70%) and tend to be old themselves (50% over age 65). Soldo also found that half of the caregving to the care recipient is by the spouse him/herself, and that, of these female caregivers, 39% are spouses, and about 41% of them 65 years of age or older. Again, a wife is most likely to be the caregiver in households where elderly couples live alone. Policy recommendations by the New York State Office for the Aging are included.

Newman, Evelyn S., Susan R. Sherman and Claire E. Higgins. Retirement Expectations and Plans: a Comparison of Professional Men and Women. In: Szinovacz, Maximiliane, ed. WOMEN'S RETIREMENT: POLICY IMPLICATIONS OF RECENT RESEARCH. Beverly Hills, California, Sage Publications, 1982. pp. 113-122.

Research based on 958 faculty and non-teaching professionals in three New York State institutions of higher education. Despite the fact that the males in this study had higher levels of income and higher status job titles than the females, gender differences in attitudes and planning were not great. University professionals in general, especially among the faculty, desired to continue working. Financial issues were a major retirement concern, even for well-paid individuals. Older female professionals were apprehensive that the greater leisure time of retirement would become a problem.

Non-Governmental Organizations. Committee on Aging. AFFIRMING LIFE: PERSPECTIVES ON AGING: REPORT TO WORLD ASSEMBLY ON AGING FROM THE NGO COMMITTEES ON AGING. New York, January 1982. 41 pp.

Among the summaries of papers presented at earlier monthly meetings, several include women in their concerns, and one in particular, L. M. Rhodes, WOMEN AGING, is directed to public policies toward the growing numbers of aged women. In the list of [international] Non-Governmental Organizations (pp. 37-41), 23 are international women's organizations which include the older woman in their sphere of interest.

Norman, Dennis K., Michael Murphy, Carol Gilligan and Jyotsna Vasudev. Sex Differences and Interpersonal Relationships: a Cross-Sectional Sample in the U.S. and India. INTERNATIONAL JOURNAL OF AGING AND HUMAN DEVELOPMENT. 14(4):291-306 (1981-1982)

This is research based on interviews with 62 persons, Indian and American, on the importance and kinds of relationships men and women make and their frequency, time of establishment and their duration in the life span. From age 19-31 women named more relationships than men; after 35 they seemed about the same. Most tables by sex and cultural origin.

Norman, William H. and Thomas J. Scaramella. MID-LIFE DEVELOPMENTAL AND CLINICAL ISSUES. New York, Brunner/Mazel Publishers, 1980. 189 pp.

This book is intended to provide the reader with a survey of the accumulating literature on the social and personal facets of this dynamic and complex period of life, and to alert the reader to developmental challenges, options and problem areas. Most chapters have some useful thoughts on women and midlife issues, but one chapter is especially directed to women, "Changing Roles for Women at Mid-Life," by Malkah Tolpin Notman (pp. 85-109, abstracted separately in this bibliography).

North American Regional Technical Meeting on Aging, Washington, D.C., June 15-16, 1981. AGING IN NORTH AMERICA: PROJECTIONS AND POLICIES. Washington, D.C., National Council on the Aging, Inc., 1982. 264 pp.

This collection of working group summaries (and the final North American recommendations of Canada and the U.S.) to the World Assembly on Aging speaks mostly of elderly persons, or "the elderly" or the "elderly worker," or even families. There is little specific mention of elderly women in the working groups (except in the report from Dolores Davis-Wong on "The National Caucus and Center on the Black Aged," pp. 47-48). One recommendation states that special attention should be given "to the problems that face present and future older women" (see p. 201). Recommendations to the United States government included specifically the need for including research and policy for aging women. The demographic profile for the United States contains tables which are mostly by sex (see A-4, A-5, B-1, C-2, D-1 and D-2).

Notelovitz, Morris and Marsha Ware. STAND TALL! THE INFORMED WOMAN'S GUIDE TO
     PREVENTING OSTEOPOROSIS. Gainesville, Florida, Triad Publishing Co.,
     1982. 208 pp.

     This book is an analysis in layman's language of osteoporosis, a
     condition usually associated with older women--one out of four having
     it. The book has many suggestions for avoiding the disease, stressing
     especially early prevention.

Notman, Malkah Tolpin. Changing Roles for Women at Mid-Life. In: Norman,
     William H. and Thomas J. Scaramella, eds. MID-LIFE: DEVELOPMENTAL AND
     CLINICAL ISSUES. New York, Brunner/Mazel, Publishers, 1980. pp. 85-
     109.

     Within the past decade, the middle years have come to be recognized as a
     time of development and growth rather than one where the major dynamic is
     toward aging and death. Nevertheless, aging continues to be dreaded in a
     culture which emphasizes youth. Women still look upon menopause as a ter-
     mination rather than a change. The major focus of this paper is on change
     and adaptation, rather than loss and decline. It addresses the changing
     roles of women at mid-life, stemming from menopause; separation from
     children; and re-entry to the work force.

Nudel, Adele. FOR THE WOMAN OVER 50. New York, Taplinger Publishing Co., 1978.
     435 pp.

     A practical guide for a full and vital life, discussing the problems the
     older woman faces, with practical suggestions for meeting them: the
     maturing body; health and the best medical care; personal appearance;
     social and marital relations; aged parents; widowhood; careers; continuing
     education; volunteering; and satisfying retirement living. Includes ten
     pages of references and a directory of agencies concerned with the aging.

Nye, Miriam Baker. BUT I NEVER THOUGHT HE'D DIE: PRACTICAL HELP FOR WIDOWS.
     Philadelphia, Westminster Press, 1978. 150 pp.

     Guide for widows: how to face widowhood, understand its feelings; identify
     and carry out the developmental tasks for emerging from these feelings;
     and set new goals following the death of the spouse.

O'Farrell, Brendan. PENSIONS AND DIVORCE: RIGHTS OF DIVORCED SPOUSES AS THEY
     PERTAIN TO PENSION BENEFITS EARNED IN THE COURSE OF EMPLOYMENT DURING
     MARRIAGE. Washington, D.C., President's Commission on Pension Policy,
     1980. 41 pp.

     Retirement income for divorced homemakers or wives of low-earning spouses
     is frequently so low that these women make up a substantial part of the
     elderly poor. State courts have made various decisions, but, until
     recently, have not considered pensions to be property. This paper con-
     centrates particularly on the factors to be considered in pension rights,
     both legal and actuarial, in divorce.

Ohio. State University, Columbus. Center for Human Resources Research.
       DUAL CAREERS: A DECADE OF CHANGES IN THE LIVES OF MATURE WOMEN, Vol. 5.
       Ed. by Lois B. Shaw. Columbus, 1981. 268 pp.

    Earlier volumes issued with the subtitle: A Longitudinal Study of Labor
    Market Experience of Women. These papers (as in preceding volumes) are
    based on interviews with the mature women's sample of the larger National
    Longitudinal Surveys (Studies) of Work Experience (four different surveys
    in all) begun by the Department of Labor in the late 1960s. The original
    sample of the mature women's survey consisted of 5,000 women, represen-
    tative, non-institutionalized, civilians aged 30-44, interviewed for the
    first time in 1967, for the seventh time in 1977. Most were married and
    40% had pre-school children in the original survey. This is a two-year
    report of the ways in which white and black women managed their employment
    careers and their households. Considerable attention is given to wives'
    perceptions of the attitudes of their husbands to their employment.
    Society became more supportive of women's work outside the home during
    these years (30% of the whites and 40% of the blacks worked steadily);
    and, for those continuously employed, there was some progress toward better
    paying work. Despite this, single female heads of families consti-
    tuted a large portion of persons at or below the poverty level.

O'Laughlin, Kay. The Final Challenge: Facing Death. In: Markson, Elizabeth W.,
       ed. OLDER WOMEN: ISSUES AND PROSPECTS. Lexington, Massachusetts,
       Lexington Books, D.C. Heath & Co., 1983. pp. 275-296.

    In her old age, a woman may experience one or several of the losses of
    that stage of her life: death of her husband; the earlier mothering role;
    retirement from a career; health; and social connections. Her final
    challenge is to contemplate her death. The denial of death and mourning
    in our society today is harmful, and professionals should seek ways and
    opportunities to remedy this gap in counseling. Widow-to-widow groups
    have made some contribution here.

Older Women's League Educational Fund. GROWING NUMBERS, GROWING FORCE: A REPORT
       FROM THE WHITE HOUSE MINI-CONFERENCE ON OLDER WOMEN. Oakland, California,
       1981. 56 pp.

    This mini-conference was convened by the League and the Western Gerontolo-
    gical Society, at Des Moines, Iowa, Oct. 9-10, 1980, the first White
    House Conference event to focus solely on concerns of middle-aged and
    older women. Participants worked from "Issue Papers" covering 15 topics
    that have impact on the lives of older women. The topics were grouped
    into three clusters: insuring adequate income; health concerns of older
    women; and quality of life and the impact of aging. Recommendations
    in all 15 areas of interest are included within the summarized discussions.
    A special panel discussion was held on minority women.

Older Women's League Educational Fund. HOW TO TAME THE CETA BEAST: AN ADVOCACY
MANUAL FOR OLDER WOMEN. Cartoons by Bulbul. Oakland, California,
September 1979. 92 pp. + appendices.

Describes CETA (Comprehensive Employment Training Act) and how the
middle-aged and older woman was able to take advantage of the opportunities it offered.

Older Women's League. National Office. THE "PAYOFF STAGE OF LIFE" FOR OLDER
WOMEN: A CRITIQUE OF THE WHITE HOUSE CONFERENCE ON AGING FINAL REPORT.
Oakland, California, July 1982. 8 pp. Prepared by Alice Quinlan.

Vol. 1 of the Final Report of the White House Conference on Aging (in
3 Vols.) contains the United States national policy on aging built on the
findings, comments, and recommendations of the Conference itself. But it
completely ignores the recommendations of Committee 11 on the Concerns of
Older Women as to Social Security, pensions, employment, housing, health
care, and other issues. The League suggests the report is essentially
political and is based on the "rugged individualism" theory without
appropriate allowances for variation in women's earlier work history and
difficulties in providing retirement income.

Olson, Sandra K. Current Status of Corporate Retirement Preparation Programs.
AGING AND WORK. 4(3):175-187 (Summer 1981)

Update of an earlier (1974) review of the literature from the last six
years on retirement preparation in private industry. Two pages are
devoted to the lesser ability of women to plan their retirement, particularly financial planning.

O'Neill, June A. and Douglas A. Wolf. MALE-FEMALE DIFFERENCES IN RETIREMENT
INCOME: THE ROLE OF PRIVATE PENSIONS. Washington, D.C., Urban Institute,
May 1982. 135 pp. + appendices.

The projected 65+ population in 1990 is 31,557,000. Of that total 65+
population, 60.1% will be women, 39.9% men. Of that same total 65+
population, 27.8% will be women over 75 years old, 14.7% men over 75 years
old (see Table 1, p. 2). The aging of the population has particular
significance for public policy because of the increasing percentage of the
Federal budget targeted on the elderly, and policy choices which will be
shaped by perceptions of the income situation of the elderly. This study,
then, reviews the current economic status and sources of income of the
elderly, and examines in detail the determinants of private pension
receipt (one important private source of support in retirement). The analysis focuses particularly on elderly women who are disproportionately
represented in public aid programs for the elderly both because of their
numerical superiority in the aged population and because they are disproportionately poor. There are 31 supporting tables in the text and 23 in
the appendices, most of them by sex. Bibliography (5 pp. at end).

O'Neill, June A. and Rachel Braun. WOMEN AND THE LABOR MARKET: A SURVEY OF ISSUES AND POLICIES IN THE UNITED STATES. Washington, D.C., Urban Institute, November 1981. 144 pp. + Statistical Supplement (issued separately, unpaged, 32 tables).

This survey paper provides research and current data and insights on 1980s role of women in the labor force. The depth and extent of this research is unmatched in current literature. The background is laid out in the first chapter, "Development of Women's Labor Force Participation in the U.S." In that chapter and the two following, "Current Patterns of Reemployment and Unemployment" and "The Earnings Differential," the role of the older woman worker is given modest attention, the purpose of the report as a whole being to cover the subject of all women in the labor force. Of the 29 tables in the first three sections, nine include the older woman in the statistics.

O'Rand, Angela M. and John C. Henretta. Delayed Career Entry, Industrial Pension Structure, and Early Retirement in a Cohort of Unmarried Women. AMERICAN SOCIOLOGICAL REVIEW. 47(3):365-373. (June 1982)

The effects of early family and work patterns and industrial pension structures on the timing of retirement among unmarried women (never married, separated, divorced, or widowed) are examined within a life course perspective. The retirement process is viewed in a longitudinal framework with similar combinations of factors influencing successive stages of final withdrawal from work.

O'Rand, Angela M. and John C. Henretta. Midlife Work History and Retirement Income. In: Szinovacz, Maximiliane, ed. WOMEN'S RETIREMENT: POLICY IMPLICATIONS OF RECENT RESEARCH. Beverly Hills, California, Sage Publications, 1982. pp. 25-44.

Studies the influence of varying work patterns of older unmarried and married women on what they expected their work life to yield in retirement income. Survey data from the ten-year Longitudinal Retirement History Study of the Social Security Administration (begun in 1969) were used to compare the income expectations of these two groups of women who were already approaching retirement age in 1969, taking into consideration the family background, work pattern, and retirement income expectations of each woman at that time. The authors point out that an adequate retirement income normally accrues from steady work over many years, a job with good wages and benefits, and good pension plans, and that women are disadvantaged, compared to men, in these three requirements for a good retirement income from one's work life.

O'Rand, Angela M. and John C. Henretta. Women at Middle Age: Developmental Transitions. ANNALS OF THE AMERICAN ACADEMY OF POLITICAL AND SOCIAL SCIENCES. 464:57-64. (November 1982)

Declining fertility, extended longevity, new life-styles in marriage and family formation, and increased participation in the labor force are shaping women's lives in the twentieth century. The author discusses future prospects for today's middle-aged women, as a consequence of these

Osgood, Nancy J., ed. LIFE AFTER WORK: RETIREMENT, LEISURE, RECREATION, AND THE ELDERLY. New York, Praeger, 1982. 367 pp.

This book is the outgrowth of a 1981 conference on "Life After Work," held at the Cortland State University of New York. Part 2 is on "Work, Retirement, and Leisure," and Section 1 (of Part 2) is a comparison of men and women, presented in three articles (all abstracted separately in this bibliography): Davidson, Janice, "Issues of Employment and Retirement in the Lives of Women Over Age 40"; Paul, Carolyn E., "Public Policy and the Work Life of Older Women"; and McGuire, Francis A., "Leisure Time, Activities, and Meanings: a Comparison of Men and Women in Late Life".

Palmer, Mary H. Assisting the Older Woman With Cosmetics. JOURNAL OF GERONTOLOGICAL NURSING. 8(2):340-342 (February 1982)

Article gives historical background of use of cosmetics; physiological changes of the skin; implications of aging for the skin (wrinkling, sagging, folding and dryness); and cosmetics and measures suitable to maintaining and improving the skin.

Papalia-Finlay, Diane, et al. Attitudes of Older Women Toward Continuing Adult Education at the University Level: Implications for Program Curriculum Development. EDUCATIONAL GERONTOLOGY. 7(2/3):159-166 (September/October 1981)

This study was conducted to examine the attitudes of potential elderly women participants in formal learning situations, to uncover their program interests, and thus provide them those programs that consider their attitudes, learning interests and needs. This survey is based on 27 white upper middle-class, highly educated women, age 65 years and over, and the results are not necessarily applicable to less economically, occupationally, and educationally privileged elderly.

Parham, Iris, et al. Widowhood Peer Counseling. AGING. No. 307/308:42-46 (May/June 1980)

Description of the widowhood peer counseling program at Virginia Center on Aging.

Parnes, Herbert S. UNEMPLOYMENT EXPERIENCE OF INDIVIDUALS OVER A DECADE: VARIATIONS BY SEX, RACE AND AGE. Kalamazoo, Michigan, W.E. Upjohn Institute for Employment Research, 1982. 99 pp.

An analysis of the unemployment experience of four subsets of the U.S. labor force, based on the National Longitudinal Surveys of Labor Market Experience. Two of the subsets were females, ages 26-34 and 40-54. Data were available for a period of eight years, from which it was evident that all these females had experienced some unemployment in this period, an idleness that reduced their earning capacity (and income). Among the strongest and most consistent characteristics which determined employment status of women were educational attainment, occupational and industrial affiliation, inter-firm mobility, and tenure in the job held at the

Patrick, Clifford H. and Edgar F. Borgatta, eds. Available Data Bases for
        Aging Research. RESEARCH ON AGING. 3(4):371-501 (December 1981)

        Special issue of the journal devoted to the presentation of some investi-
        gations that describe and indicate directions for the use of some of the
        larger data sets in the field of aging. Two pertinent papers are: Lola W.
        Irelan and Karen Schwab, "Social Security Administration's Retirement
        History Study" (pp. 381-386), with conclusions by sex; and Joan F. Van
        Nostrand, "Aged in Nursing Homes: Baseline Data" (pp. 403-415), with some
        information by sex.

Paul, Carolyn E. Public Policy and the Work Life of Older Women. In: Osgood,
        Nancy J., ed. LIFE AFTER WORK: RETIREMENT, LEISURE, RECREATION, AND THE
        ELDERLY. New York, Praeger, 1982. pp. 119-131.

        Early retirement is resulting in escalating costs to public and private
        pension programs, costs which have arisen from liberalization of pension
        coverage and demographic changes in the working population. Little has
        been written yet of the consequences for older females of the suggested
        policy proposals for slowing these rising costs. This article explores
        this issue, recognizing that data assessing the impact are scarce, and
        highlights differences that may result in the future involvement of women
        in the work force.

Peace, Sheila M. INTERNATIONAL PERSPECTIVE ON THE STATUS OF OLDER WOMEN.
        Washington, D.C., International Federation on Ageing, 1981. 92 pp.
        (Prepared as a background paper for the U.N. World Conference "Decade for
        Women," Copenhagen, July 1980)

        Because the majority of recommendations from the 1975 International Women's
        Year Conference at Mexico City concerned young and middle-aged women, an
        attempt is made here to redress that earlier oversight of older women.
        The present paper addresses itself to roles and images of older women;
        demographic and sociological profile of older women; women and family
        related roles; health and older women; and income, pensions and Social
        Security. There are numerous tables.

Pearldaughter, Andra, Virginia Dean, Frances Leonard and Tish Sommers. WELFARE:
        END OF THE LINE FOR WOMEN. Washington, D.C., Older Women's League, May
        1980. 20 pp. (Gray Paper, No. 5)

        This paper discusses the roots of poverty in older women despite Social
        Security, pension systems and individual savings, and offers ideas for
        improvement. Older black, Hispanic and native American women are more
        disadvantaged than other older American women. The roots of this poverty
        lie in women's participation in the traditional homemaker role and/or in
        low paid employment. Women's longer life expectancy and intermittent
        labor force participation contribute to the older woman's poverty,
        obliging many to depend on welfare and small Social Security benefits, if
        any.

Pellegrino, Victoria Y. OTHER SIDE OF THIRTY. New York, Rawson, Wade
    Publishers, Inc., 1981. 241 pp.

    This book is directed especially to the woman between 30 and 40 years of
    age, but discusses problems and issues similar to those the older woman
    faces: divorce, personal growth and freedom, new job, and societal and
    governmental changes. Bibliography: pp. 223-236.

Peterson, David A. Participation in Education by Older People. EDUCATIONAL
    GERONTOLOGY. 7(2/3):245-256 (September/October 1981)

    Current knowledge on the encouragements and constraints affecting
    educational participation by older people. Participation given
    separately for men and women.

Porcino, Jane. GROWING OLDER, GETTING BETTER: A HANDBOOK FOR WOMEN IN THE
    SECOND HALF OF LIFE. Reading, Massachusetts, Addison-Wesley Publishing
    Co., 1983. 364 pp.

    In her foreword, Maggie Kuhn calls Porcino's book a unique and useful
    handbook for the encouragement and empowerment of women in midlife and
    late life, a handbook to share with other women (and men) who are aging.
    Pt. 1 takes up the woman in this transition period of her life: family,
    marital status, and crises thereto; new "paths" to be explored and taken;
    different living arrangements; woman's place in the work force; achieve-
    ment of good mental health. Pt. 2 discusses a woman's changing body:
    menopause; sexuality; osteoporosis; other diseases and afflictions of the
    older woman; alcoholism and drug abuse; and the high cost of good health
    care and health insurance. Each chapter is replete with statistics,
    quotations (mostly anonymous) illustrative of the text, and resources at
    the end (bibliography and organizations).

Price-Bonham, Sharon and Carolyn Kitchings Johnson. Attitudes Toward
    Retirement: a Comparison of Professional and Nonprofessional Married
    Women. In: Szinovacz, Maximiliane, ed. WOMEN'S RETIREMENT: POLICY
    IMPLICATIONS OF RECENT RESEARCH. Beverly Hills, California, Sage
    Publications, 1982. pp. 123-138.

    Major purpose of the study was to compare professional and nonprofessional
    women's attitudes toward retirement and to explore characteristics that
    contribute to positive attitudes. Data were collected on ten variables,
    none of which seemed to relate significantly to retirement attitudes of
    the nonprofessional except reliance on the husband's retirement benefits.
    Professional women had the stronger job commitment and were significantly
    less likely to feel positive about retirement as a result, unless they
    anticipated continuing to work beyond retirement.

Puglisi, J. Thomas and Dorothy W. Jackson. Sex Role Identity and Self-Esteem in Adulthood. INTERNATIONAL JOURNAL OF AGING AND HUMAN DEVELOPMENT. 12(2):129-138 (1980-1981)

This research, based on participation by 1,029 males and 1,040 females, 17 to 89 years old and reported by decades, indicates that persons having both male and female characteristics have the highest self-esteem; and conversely, those "undifferentiated" individuals score lowest in self-esteem. Masculinity was a better predictor of self-esteem than was femininity. The hypothesis of a convergence of sex-role characteristics in later life was not supported.

Pursell, Donald E. and William D. Torrence. The Older Woman and Her Search for Employment. AGING AND WORK. 3(2):121-128 (Spring 1980)

The unemployment duration and post-unemployment earnings of older women unemployed in October 1976.

Quayhagen, Mary P. and Margaret Quayhagen. Coping With Conflict: Measurement of Age-Related Patterns. RESEARCH ON AGING. 4(3):364-377 (September 1982)

The Coping Strategies Inventory was developed to provide an age-relevant measure of coping responses to specified stress situations. In this age-stratified sample of mid-life adults (77 men and 141 women), age and sex differences were found in specific coping patterns used to alter the interpersonal conflict situation and related stress.

Quinn, Joseph F. Wage Determination and Discrimination Among Older Workers. JOURNAL OF GERONTOLOGY. 34(5):728-735 (September 1979)

Analysis was made of wage determinants and the extent of race and sex discrimination among older workers. Much of the seeming discrimination against women is accounted for by the fact that they are mainly in the lower paying jobs.

Rathbone-McCuan, Eloise and Joan Hashimi. ISOLATED ELDERS: HEALTH AND SOCIAL INTERVENTION. Rockville, Maryland, Aspen Publications, 1982. 324 pp.

Authors discuss the major factors which lead to isolation (isolators) among the elderly. Ch. 3, "Older and Elderly Women: Survivors into Isolation" (pp. 27-57), discusses the serious condition of older women and the services available to them, presently uncoordinated, for their physical, psychological, and social problems. The index is useful in separating materials by sex.

Rathbone-McCuan, Eloise and Vicki Hart. A Pilot Training Program in the Mental Health of Older Women. EDUCATIONAL GERONTOLOGY. 6(4):353-363 (June 1981)

Description and analysis of a pilot social work education program in the mental health of older women. Presents results of a five-year study.

Rawlings, Steve W. Families Maintained by Female Householders, 1970-1979.
    CURRENT POPULATION REPORTS, SERIES P-23 (SPECIAL STUDIES), No. 107,
    October 1980. 49 pp.

    This special study presents tables by age on: living arrangements;
    demographic characteristics; income, etc. of households maintained by
    females aged 14-75+.

Reedy, Margaret Neiswender. Personality and Aging. In: Woodruff, Diana S.
    and James E. Birren, eds. AGING: SCIENTIFIC PERSPECTIVES AND SOCIAL
    ISSUES. 2d ed. Monterey, California, Brooks/Cole Publishing Co., 1983.
    pp. 112-136.

    In this discussion of personality and aging, there is a small section on
    "cohort and sex differences in personality" (pp. 123-124), in which the
    author acknowledges the paucity of information on how the sexes differ in
    their personality adjustments to aging, and cites some seven earlier stu-
    dies on this aspect of aging. She does suggest that, with the current
    cultural emphasis on male parenting and female labor force participation,
    the sex role reversal we see in older retired couples today may be less
    likely to occur as today's young people grow older.

Reno, Virginia and Anne Dee Rader. Benefits for Individual Retired Workers and
    Couples Now Approaching Retirement Age. SOCIAL SECURITY BULLETIN. 45(2):
    25-31 (February 1982)

    Focuses on the potential full retired-worker/Social Security benefits
    to be earned by men and women reaching retirement age in the early 1980s.
    An increasing proportion of married women will become insured for bene-
    fits in their own right; but, among female workers, the highest benefits
    are projected for those who never married. Tables by sex and/or marital
    status.

Research and Forecasts, Inc. REPORT ON AGING IN AMERICA: TRIALS AND TRIUMPHS.
    Monticello, Illinois, Americana Healthcare Corporation, 1980. 105 pp.

    The subtitle of this survey is "A Unique and Revealing National Study
    of America's Burgeoning 60-Plus Population: Subjective Views, Objective
    Realities." Text, graphs and statistics frequently present sex differen-
    ces in reporting on how the 60+ population feel about themselves and their
    world, and how they cope with change. The sample divided the findings
    into three groups: enjoyers (27% of sample), survivors (53% of sample),
    and casualties (20% of sample). This last group, hardest hit by age-
    related difficulties, is predominantly female, poorly educated, and in
    fair to poor health, with low assets and household income.

Richards, Mary Lynne. The Clothing Preferences and Problems of Elderly Female
    Consumers. GERONTOLOGIST. 21(3):263-267 (June 1981)

    Female members of organizations for elders in western Texas responded to
    questionnaires about preferences for and problems with ready-made dresses.

Riddick, Carol Cutler. Life Satisfaction Among Aging Women: a Causal Model.
In: Szinovacz, Maximiliane, ed. WOMEN'S RETIREMENT: POLICY IMPLICATIONS
OF RECENT RESEARCH. Beverly Hills, California, Sage Publications, 1982.
pp. 45-59.

Through the use of earlier research, the author draws up a theoretical
model for the life satisfaction of older females with labor force
background, selecting variables that could contribute to understanding and
explaining life satisfaction: employment status; health problems; income;
transportation barriers; and friendship, voluntary association affiliation, and solitary recreational activity. Of all the variables considered, leisure roles had the strongest positive relationship with life
satisfaction.

Riley, Matilda White. Implications for the Middle and Later Years. In:
Berman, Phyllis W. and Estelle R. Ramey, eds. WOMEN: A DEVELOPMENTAL
PERSPECTIVE. Washington, D.C., U.S. Government Printing Office, 1982.
pp. 399-411.

Riley briefly reviews other research papers in these proceedings of the
first National Institutes of Health Research Conference on the Concerns
of Women, and applies these findings to women in the middle and older
years. She points out that old age is part of the total life course and
is affected by social change. Older women living through these
experiences, the author predicts, will, in the future, have developed
greater independence and self-reliance because of current social changes.

Riley, Matilda White. Old Women: a Gerontologist Maintains That Old Age Can
Be a Time of Creativity and Service. RADCLIFFE QUARTERLY. June 1979.
pp. 7-10.

Riley maintains that the 13 million women age 65 and over have more to
offer society than society is ready to receive, and more of themselves to
offer than they believe possible, despite their double disadvantage (that
they are old, and beyond that, old women). This low acceptance of older
women indicates there is something wrong with the social arrangements of
our time which neglect their education and work backgrounds. The male/
female ratio in the older population (and accompanying longer life
expectancy) opens up the need to consider the place of the older woman in
the changing social picture where this older population is disproportionately women, most of them widows. Riley discusses some earlier
barriers which excluded women from traditional male roles, and how these
barriers are "coming down."

Rogers, Gayle Thompson. Aged Widows and OASDI: Age at and Economic Status
Before and After Receipt of Benefits. SOCIAL SECURITY BULLETIN. 44(3):
3-19 (March 1981)

Based on panel data from the Retirement History Study, this paper analyzes
the economic status of widows in late middle age. It proposes to describe
the income, labor-force, and demographic characteristics of widows before
they become eligible for benefits; to examine the age at which they elect

OASDI benefits (Old Age, Survivors, and Disability Insurance) and the characteristics associated with that decision; and to compare their economic status before and after they begin collecting benefits. Employment during the pre-OASDI period greatly influenced a widow's benefit-timing decision.

Rogers, Natalie. EMERGING WOMAN: A DECADE OF MIDLIFE TRANSITIONS. Point Reyes, California, Personal Press, 1980. 201 pp.

The chapter on "Sex Roles During Separation and Divorce" discusses the trauma and many life adjustments in suddenly being single. Part one of "The Impact of Women on My Life" presents the impact of the older, traditional woman on the modern mature woman.

Rones, Philip L. Aging of the Older Population and the Effect on Its Labor Force Rates. MONTHLY LABOR REVIEW. 105(9):27-29 (September 1982)

The labor force participation rates for older women have changed comparatively little over time according to population and labor force data from the Current Population Survey for 1968, 1972, and 1981. But, in the years ahead, the aging of the first generation of American women who have developed a strong labor force attachment is likely to change these rates upward for women age 55 and over. Table by age/sex.

Rose, Helen. BEGIN TO LIVE. New York, St. Martin's Press, 1979. 186 pp.

Guide to retirement living for people over 50, illustrated with case histories, many of which are from or about women.

Rosen, Ellen. Beyond the Sweatshop: Older Women in Blue-Collar Jobs. In: Markson, Elizabeth W., ed. OLDER WOMEN: ISSUES AND PROSPECTS. Lexington, Massachusetts, Lexington Books, D.C. Heath & Co., 1983. pp. 75-91.

Explores the work experiences of female factory workers in New England and the ways in which current employment conditions shape their lives. Almost half the women in this study were age 45 or older. The past decade has seen significant increases in the number of blue-collar jobs held by women, especially in Massachusetts. The author notes that many women dropped out of the World War II work force to raise children, re-entering perhaps ten or fifteen years later. Their work patterns showed a remarkable continuity of participation in the labor force from then on, except for lay-offs and other instabilities in the employment world. These work-life gaps prove traumatic in that they lead to reduced pension benefits.

Rubin, Lillian B. WOMEN OF A CERTAIN AGE: THE MIDLIFE SEARCH FOR SELF. New York, Harper and Row, 1979. 309 pp.

A book derived from the author's own experience and from interviews with 160 women who ranged in age from 35 to 54, about changes in life, family, and career for midlife women. Bibliography: pp. 262-302.

Rytina, Nancy F. Occupational Changes and Tenure, 1981. MONTHLY LABOR REVIEW, 105(9):29-33 (September 1982)

Table one shows occupational mobility during 1981 by age/sex, by groups up to age 55-64, and then by age 65+. Table two, on reasons for occupational change, is again by age/sex, and the same age ranges. Some text by sex/age.

Sandos, James Daniel. The Relationship of Stressful Life Events to Intellectual Functioning in Women Over 65. INERNATIONAL JOURNAL OF AGING AND HUMAN DEVEOPMENT. 14(1):11-23 (1981-82)

Utility of stress scales to estimate decline in intellectual abilities of elderly women (age 65-92) is questioned, as it may result in the masking of specific relationships between behavior and environmental events, especially personal health or changes in the health of a family member.

Sauer, Herbert I. Geographic Patterns in the Risk of Dying and Associated Factors, Ages 35-74 Years, United States, 1968-1972. VITAL AND HEALTH STATISTICS, SER. 3, ANALYTICAL STUDIES, No. 18, September 1980. 120 pp.

This study, from the National Center for Health Statistics, analyzes mortality rates from natural causes, malignant neoplasms (colo-rectal cancer, pancreatic cancer, respiratory cancer, breast cancer), cardiovascular diseases, and chronic respiratory diseases. Almost half of the text figures and tables present the information by age/sex. Various factors in the environment are considered in associating the geographic patterns with the risk of dying in that area.

Schutz, Howard G., Pamela C. Baird and Glenn R. Hawkes. LIFESTYLES AND CONSUMER BEHAVIOR OF OLDER AMERICANS. New York, Praeger, 1979. 276 pp.

In this survey of lifestyle patterns among older men and women and the relation of the lifestyle to consumer behavior, the text treats most characteristics as common to men and women. However, Table 1.2 (pp. 10-15), "Female Interests and Opinions, by Age Groups," lists a series of statements in various categories: optimism and happiness; travel; mobility; anxiety; personal adornment; income and spending; durable goods; housekeeping, grocery shopping; health, and nutrition; and what percentage agreed with the statement. In general, age with or without the consideration of sex was not highly related to consumer behavior.

Scott, Jean Pearson and Vira R. Kivett. Widowed, Black Older Adult in the Rural South: Implications for Policy. FAMILY RELATIONS. January 1980. pp. 83-90.

Study of 72 rural black elderly widows with respect to a number of characteristics, such as health, income, education, home ownership, transportation, and organizations to which they belonged. These elderly black widows were more disadvantaged than other rural women, although church and family were major supporters of both groups. Delivery of services to the elderly black widow at the local level should be improved.

Segalla, Rosemary Anastasio. DEPARTURE FROM TRADITIONAL ROLES: MID-LIFE WOMEN
     BREAK THE DAISY CHAINS. Ann Arbor, Michigan, UMI Research Press, 1982.
     151 pp. (Research in Clinical Psychology, No. 5)

     This book reviews the position of women in post-World War II. The author
     posits that the young woman of the 1950's at the time of this writing had
     become a mid-life woman--highly educated for a career outside the home,
     succeeding academically, ambitious, but dominated and directed by the world-
     wide societal belief that marriage and family was the career first, among
     all other careers, to be elected on graduation from college. Typically,
     utilization of her education for a second career (outside the home) was to
     be postponed until the children were able to be on their own. The
     purpose of this study is to understand the current life styles of six
     groups of 76 educated women (between 35 and 45, all married with the
     youngest child still in school), as they departed from the traditional
     career role of homemaker and entered alternative life styles.

Seltzer, Mildred M. The Older Woman: Fact, Fantasies, and Fiction. RESEARCH
     ON AGING. 1(2):139-154 (June 1979)

     Research on the older woman is an outgrowth of two major sociocultural
     trends: 1) the women's movement itself, and 2) the succeeding greying of
     America. The mid-20th century resurgence of the woman's movement was pre-
     eminently a young woman's movement which gave lesser attention to the
     "older sister." This inattention began to change in the 1970s, when the
     1950s woman herself had become an older sister. Seltzer traces the
     increasing interest in the older woman by citing conferences, per-
     sonalities, funding, films and publications. She summarizes the current
     information in seven categories and cites the literature of each: 1) pole-
     mic research; 2) men/women comparisons; 3) sex-role empiricism; 4)
     historical and cross-cultural analysis; 5) heuristic essays and papers;
     6) "happiness" aspect of growing older; and 7) popular literature on
     aging.

Selzer, S. Clair and Nancy Wadsworth Denney. Conservation Abilities in Middle-
     Aged and Elderly Adults. INTERNATIONAL JOURNAL OF AGING AND HUMAN
     DEVELOPMENT. 11(2):135-146 (1980)

     The conservation abilities of middle-aged and elderly adults were tested
     (in three areas: substance, weight, and volume) and compared. In this
     study, sex made no significant difference. Table by sex.

Serow, William J. Consideration on the Present and Future Well-being of Older
     Americans. In: Institute on Minority Aging, 7th, San Diego, California,
     February 6-8, 1980. MINORITY AGING: POLICY ISSUES FOR THE '80s. Ed. by
     E. Percil Stanford. San Diego, Campanile Press, 1981. pp. 11-20.

     In the first part of this short paper, Serow deals with trends in the
     economic status of older persons in terms of employment and labor force
     participation, income, and sources of income. Women are surveyed briefly
     as part of labor force (see Table 2, p. 14), and the poverty position of
     female-headed households (Table 4, p. 16).

Shanas, Ethel. Family as a Social Support System in Old Age. GERONTOLOGIST. 19(2):169-174 (April 1979)

In this report on two aspects of the family as a social support system (family care for the elderly in illness, and family visiting patterns), the role of the elderly wife or husband is also highlighted in such areas as housework, meal preparation and shopping (see Table 3).

Shaw, Lois Banfill. Causes of Irregular Employment Patterns. In: Shaw, Lois B., ed. UNPLANNED CAREERS: THE WORKING LIVES OF MIDDLE-AGED WOMEN. Lexington, Massachusetts, Lexington Books, 1982. pp. 45-59.

Middle-aged and married women are not continuously employed for such reasons as family, health, personal choice, state of unemployment in their area, all of which affect earnings. This work pattern and low wages may hamper her search for steady work when the need arises in her later life.

Shaw, Lois Banfill. Problems of Labor-Market Reentry. In: Shaw, Lois B., ed. UNPLANNED CAREERS: THE WORKING LIVES OF MIDDLE-AGED WOMEN. Lexington, Massachusetts, Lexington Books, 1982. pp. 33-44.

Discusses the problems (from 1966-1977) of reentry of women to the labor force after a long absence. Unemployment in their area did not seem to discourage women from reentry. Younger women were slightly more likely to reenter than older ones; there was no evidence of age discrimination, nor did older women have lower wages than younger ones.

Shaw, Lois Banfill, ed. UNPLANNED CAREERS: THE WORKING LIVES OF MIDDLE-AGED WOMEN. Lexington, Massachusetts, Lexington Books, 1982. 149 pp.

Based on continuing interviews, from 1967 to 1977, for the National Long-itudinal Survey of the Work Experience of Mature Women, beginning with 5,000 women (30-44 years of age) and ending with 4,000 of the same women (now aged 40-54). The study is especially pertinent to studying the changes in the work experience of middle-aged women in that 10-year interval: how they have fared; their problems and suggested solutions and policy implications; how secure and independent is their old age; and how their experience may help beginning young women workers plan their own career. In addition to the introduction and conclusion by the editor, there are six signed articles. (Contents abstracted separately in this bibliography):

> Shaw, Lois B. Problems of Labor-Market Reentry. pp. 33-44.
> Shaw, Lois B. Causes of Irregular Employment Patterns. pp. 45-59.
> Daymont, Thomas and Anne Statham. Occupational Atypicality: Changes, Causes, and Consequences. pp. 61-76.
> Statham, Anne and Patricia Rhoton. Attitudes Toward Women Working: Changes Over Time and Implications for the Labor-Force Behavior of Husbands and Wives. pp. 77-92.
> Chirikos, Thomas N. and Gilbert Nestel. Economic Consequences of Poor Health in Mature Women. pp. 93-108.
> Nestel, Gilbert, Jacqueline Mercier and Lois B. Shaw. Economic Consequences of Midlife Change in Marital Status. pp. 109-125.

Sheehy, Gail. PATHFINDERS. New York, William Morrow & Co., 1981. 566 pp.

Author explains that "pathfinders" are the young or old or middle-aged, from all sections of life, handicapped in one way or another, but all survivors of life's challenges and stressful events. She explores the ways in which many of these pathfinders were able to seek and find solutions, some of them uncommon solutions, to everyday or uncommon life crises. Some 60,000 men and women completed her extensive Life History Questionnaire and consented to many personal interviews. These case histories include those of many middle-aged and older women who became successful pathfinders and overcame adult life crises.

Shields, Laurie. DISPLACED HOMEMAKERS: ORGANIZING FOR A NEW LIFE. Epilogue by Tish Sommers. New York, McGraw-Hill, 1981. 272 pp.

The second part of the title states the purpose of the book: once the homemaker job is over, a woman (frequently an older woman) must re-orient her thinking and action. Volunteerism is one possibility, but a paid job is more usually the real need, often requiring further education and training, as well as a new perspective. Included is a directory, by state, of centers, programs and projects providing services to displaced (or former) homemakers.

Shock, Nathan W. Biological and Physiological Characteristics of Aging in Men and Women. In: International Conference of Social Gerontology, 9th, Quebec, August 27-28, 1980. ADAPTABILITY AND AGING, Vol. 2. Paris, International Center of Social Gerontology, May 1981. pp. 9-27.

Discusses physiological differences between males and females (length of life and mortality rates; demographic and social consequences; sex differences in longevity; and metabolic differences); sex differences in behavior and life styles; sex differences in morbidity; and future trends in mortality. Generous statistics in the text and seven tables by age/sex. The research which Shock cites basically concerns Americans.

Shock, Nathan W. Current Publications in Gerontology and Geriatrics. JOURNAL OF GERONTOLOGY. 35(6):960-986 (November 1980)

Final appearance of this feature section which has been presented in each issue of the JOURNAL OF GERONTOLOGY since Vol. 5, No. 2, 1950, and continuously edited during those 30 years by Nathan W. Shock. The unannotated listing of current materials is by author, in a classed subject arrangement which has continued unchanged throughout. The final issue each year of the Journal has included a separate author index for these materials. Dr. Shock indexed not only journal literature and monographs but also conference papers and collections of papers. Once the researcher becomes familiar with the classed subject arrangement, a patient examination of the pertinent subject groups will reward him/her beyond any first expectations, the searcher bearing in mind that only the wording of the title will reveal the pertinancy of the indexed materials. In literature on the mature and older women, as on any other subject in gerontology and geriatrics, this CURRENT PUBLICATIONS IN GERONTOLOGY AND GERIATRICS will provide a retrospective and voluminous insight into that subject.

Siegel, Jacob S. and Jeffrey S. Passel. Coverage of the Hispanic Population of the United States in the 1970 Census. CURRENT POPULATION REPORTS. SERIES P-23, (SPECIAL STUDIES), No. 82, [1979]. 43 pp.

Some eight of the 16 detailed tables give statistics by sex on the Spanish-surnamed, Hispanic, Puerto Rican, and Mexican-American population.

Siegel, Jacob S. and Cynthia M. Taeuber. The 1980 Census and the Elderly: New Data Available to Planners and Practitioners. GERONTOLOGIST. 22(2):144-150 (April 1982)

In the 1980 census, the basic demographic questions asked of all persons included age, sex, race, Hispanic origin, relationship, and marital status. In addition, another set of detailed questions was asked of a sampling of the population. Between the two sets of questions, a great deal of information has been gathered which reflects the status of the older woman in many significant areas. Many important trends and significant problems can be identified and analyzed as a consequence, and research possibilities are numerous.

Silverman, Phyllis R. HELPING WOMEN COPE WITH GRIEF. Beverly Hills, California, Sage Publications, 1981. 111 pp. (Sage Human Services Guide, 25)

This book results from research about grief which women suffer from widowhood, from physical abuse (battered women), and from the problems of unwed motherhood and illegitimacy. One of the most useful results is the recognition that grief is not a disease to be "cured," but a time of transition; a time of loss, of course, but also of gain. To regain their "wholeness," these women learn to accommodate and eventually to exist independently.

Singh, B. Krishna and J. Sherwood Williams. Childlessness and Family Satisfaction. RESEARCH ON AGING. 3(2):218-227 (June 1981)

The negative effects of childlessness on family satisfaction among older persons are more pronounced among older women than men. Statistics by sex.

Sinnott, Jan Dynda. Sex-Role Inconstancy, Biology, and Successful Aging: a Dialectical Model. In: Hendricks, Jon and C. David Hendricks, eds. DIMENSIONS OF AGING: READINGS. Cambridge, Massachusetts, Winthrop Publishers, Inc., 1979. pp. 144-149.

Sinnott seeks to extend Kline's hypothesis that the inconstancy of roles throughout the lifespan of women may account for their relative resiliance during the role changes of old age. She suggests (based on a number of studies) that a person's ability to show lifespan variations in sex roles is an indication of a general flexibility which is associated in some way with more successful aging and a longer lifespan, and offers several possible explanations for the association.

Smith, Ralph E., ed. SUBTLE REVOLUTION: WOMEN AT WORK. Washington, D.C.,
    Urban Institute, 1979. 279 pp.

    Explores the changes in our society as they affect women, specifically the
    changed needs of women relative to income, marriage, and family. It is
    noted that now women will be in the work force throughout most of their
    working years and that the majority are married with family respon-
    sibilities, trends which have special implications for the Social Security
    system as a source of retirement income of working women. See Ch. 8,
    "Institutional Responses: the Social Security System," by Nancy M. Gordon
    (abstracted separately in this bibliography).

SOCIAL INDICATORS III: SELECTED DATA ON SOCIAL CONDITIONS AND TRENDS IN THE
    UNITED STATES. Washington, D.C., U.S. Government Printing Office, 1980.
    585 pp.

    Continuation of a series of triennial reports from the Center for
    Demographic Studies, Bureau of the Census, presenting a comprehensive
    variety of statistical information picturing important aspects of the
    current social situation and underlying historical trends and develop-
    ments. The indicators relate to the total U.S. population and selected
    subgroups (sex, age group, and two broad racial categories). The tables
    and charts in certain sections give data by age/sex: population
    composition; living arrangement; marital status; health resources; life
    expectancy; health; job tenure.

Social Security Bulletin. ANNUAL STATISTICAL SUPPLEMENT, 1981. Washington, D.C.,
    U.S. Government Printing Office, 1982. 272 pp.

    The 1981 Supplement presents numerous tables on Social Security awards by
    age/sex, including Old-Age Insurance, Survivors Insurance, and Medicare
    Benefits, especially in the section of awards to retired workers.

Soldo, Beth J. America's Elderly in the 1980s. POPULATION BULLETIN. 35(4),
    November 1980. 48 pp.

    Of the 19 statistical figures and tables on today's elderly, six are by
    age/sex: labor force participation, 1947-1979; over 65, by race, 1960-2000;
    life expectancy, by race, 1900, 1950, and 1978; self-reported health status
    of the non-institutionalized, by age, 1976; marital status 65+, 1978; and
    living arrangements, by age, 1976.

Sommers, Tish. Epilogue. In: Shields, Laurie. DISPLACED HOMEMAKERS: ORGANIZ-
    ING FOR A NEW LIFE. New York, McGraw-Hill Book Co., 1981. pp. 190-216.

    The author (who herself coined the phrase "displaced homemaker" in 1974)
    reminisces on what it used to mean to be newly married and a happy
    "homemaker," and the reality that emerged in the 1970s as changes in the
    marital status deprived her of her social role, an occupation, a depen-
    dency status, and a livelihood. Sommers considers employment and economic

security high up among the objectives of programs benefitting the displaced homemaker, and outlines 10 major job-creation lessons of the late 70s and early 80s, with samples of projects that have come out of them. Sommers also discusses public policy and the older woman; Social Security; pensions; health; and myths about older women (menopause; appearance; sexuality; senility).

Sommers, Tish and Laurie Shields. OLDER WOMAN AND HEALTH CARE: STRATEGY FOR SURVIVAL. Washington, D.C., Older Women's League, January 1980. 21 pp. (Gray Paper No. 3)

This paper developed from a number of sessions of a special health commit-tee of the Older Women's League Educational Fund (OWLEF). The paper focu-ses on health concerns of older women from the menopause and after. It examines: 1) some of the conflicting concerns of health care, and proposes for each a strategy for finding a way through them; 2) the most prevalent myths about older women which plague the health care professions and the women (e.g., older women are unattractive, good health belongs to the young, age and senility are synonymous); and 3) ways in which the health care system can be improved. Resources are listed on pp. 20-21.

Sommers, Tish and Laurie Shields. OLDER WOMEN AND PENSIONS: CATCH 22. Washington, D.C., Older Women's League, January 1980. 15 pp. (Gray Paper, No. 4)

The authors state that "Pension funds in America represent one of the greatest accumulations of capital in the history of the world... Yet older American women, who comprise two-thirds of the retired population, share substantially less of this great national resource by every way of measurement. The result is that the poverty rate of women is 60% higher than that of men... This paper will point out some of the ways that sex discrimination reduces the pension income received by women, and what can be done about it..." The paper enlarges on these points under three cate-gories of older women: the homemaker; the employed woman; the survivor; and education, legislation, litigation and negotiation in their behalf.

Sommers, Tish. 1981 WHITE HOUSE CONFERENCE ON AGING: OPENING PRESENTATION TO DELEGATES ASSIGNED TO COMMITTEE #11, CONCERNS OF OLDER WOMEN, GROWING NUMBERS, SPECIAL NEEDS. Oakland, California, Older Women's League Educational Fund, 1981. 10 pp.

Special concerns of older women are described; directions for solutions of the problems, including the roles of the public and private sectors and of the individual, are suggested; and steps towards the solutions of the problems are presented.

Sommers, Tish, ed. Women and Aging. GENERATIONS. 4(4) (August 1980) 40 pp.

A collection of short papers on women and aging occupies the whole of this issue. Contents as follows:

Dunn, Tedi and Robin R. Linden. Older Women and Language. pp. 4-8.
Sommers, Tish. If We Could Write the Script. pp. 7-8, 34.
Keys, Martha. Elderly Majority: Unique Resources and Unique Needs.
   pp. 9, 35.
Star, Susan Leigh and Grace Patson. Looking Forward, Looking Back.
   pp. 10-11.
Burton, John L. Elder Women Suffer Frequently and Severely During
   Retirement. pp. 12, 36.
Cahn, Ann Foote. American Mid-Life Women: Their Unique Status and
   Prospects. pp. 13-14.
Burton, Sandra J. National Displaced Homemakers Network Promotes
   Grassroots Advocacy for Elders. pp. 15, 37.
Goodchilds, Jacqueline D. and Tora Kay Bikson. The Older Woman Living
   Alone: a Social Psychological Perspective on a Common Circumstance.
   pp. 16, 37.
Jackson, Jacquelyne Johnson. Categorical Differences of Older Black
   Women. pp. 17, 33.
Rolfe, Bari, et al. Aging on Their Own: Life Styles of Older Women.
   pp. 18-19, 38-39.
Pedrin, Verna and Sheryl Brown. Sexism and Ageism: Obstacles to
   Health Care for Women. pp. 20-21.
Hackett, Adeline. Breast Cancer Remains a Major Problem for Women.
   pp. 22-23.
Fleshman, Ruth P. and Clemmie Barry. Women Who Care for Brain-
   Damaged Husbands. pp. 24-25.
McCloud, Fiona and Elissa Van Til. Support Groups Provide Catalyst
   for Sisterhood. pp. 26-27.
Head, C.A. A Mock Report to the World Conference: the Decade of Women,
   2010. pp. 28-29, 35.
Spencer, Michael J. Resource List: Women & Aging. p. 31.

Sommers, Tish. Women and Aging: More on the Double Standard. In: Suseelan,
   M.A., ed. RESOURCE BOOK ON AGING. New York, United Church Board for
   Homeland Ministries, Health and Welfare Division, 1981. pp. 31-34.

Sommers suggests that the double standard of aging is a major inequity in
the life of women so obvious that it is taken for granted. She notes the
time disparity between the gradual aging of the man and the earlier age at
which a woman is considered "old," constituting a society of two "aging"
attitudes. She contrasts the results in retirement income, poverty, and
Social Security.

Sontag, Susan. The Double Standard of Ageing. In: Carver, Vida and Penny
   Liddiard, eds. AGEING POPULATION: A READER AND SOURCE BOOK . New York,
   Holmes & Neier Publishers, Inc., 1979. pp. 72-80.

Differentiates between the aging of men and women in such characteristics
as physical appearance, sexual feelings, and loneliness. In a society
dedicated to "youthfulness," the double standard about aging shows up
harshly in the conventions of sexual feeling, and takes for granted a
disparity between the sexes and to the woman's disadvantage. The
appearance, especially the facial appearance, of a woman is taken as an
indicator of aging, and establishes the norm of feeling toward all other
characteristics of the mature woman. Thus, for most women, aging becomes
a sad process of gradual disqualification in many of h s aspects.

Spruiell, Phyllis R. and Marion Jernigan. Clothing Preferences of Older Women: Implications for Gerontology and the American Clothing Industry. EDUCATIONAL GERONTOLOGY. 8(5):485-492 (September/October 1982)

Thirty older women (65+) were interviewed by the researchers. Opinions were collected on colors, styles, and dress features. Blue was the preferred color; styles were conservative. This investigation is of significance to clothing manufacturers, as it shows what their designers should do to meet the needs of the older female population.

Statham, Anne and Patricia Rhoton. Attitudes Toward Women Working: Changes Over Time and Implications for the Labor-Force Behaviors of Husbands and Wives. In: Shaw, Lois B. ed. UNPLANNED CAREERS: THE WORKING LIVES OF MIDDLE-AGED WOMEN. Lexington, Massachusetts, Lexington Books, 1982. pp. 77-92.

A study of attitudes toward women working over a time period of 1967-1977. The attitudes of women are a product of such factors as their own work experience and more especially the attitudes of the husbands. The latter were often more approving of their wives sharing the provider role the nearer they approached retirement. This research seemed to show that adverse attitudes toward women working are lessening, but further research is needed to show whether or not the labor force participation of women is pre-eminently a personal desire to work.

STATISTICAL BULLETIN. Issued, New York, by Metropolitan Life Foundation. Now in Vol. 64, 1983. Each issue usually about 15 pp. in length.

Statistics with text on a wide variety of subjects of interest and research value to this insurance company. The statistics are prepared from basic data often originating from other agencies, such as Bureau of the Census, National Center for Health Statistics, Decennial Census, and other private and public agencies. Anyone interested in statistics (in any area, not just the elderly) should monitor this praiseworthy publication. Some articles pertinent to this bibliography in Volumes 61-63, 1980-1982, are:

State Variations in Longevity. 61(1):10-13 (January/March 1980)
Mortality Differentials Favor Women. 61(2):3-7 (April/June 1980)
Cardiovascular Diseases--United States, Canada, and Western Europe. 61(4):8-12 (October/December 1980)
Expectation of Life in the United States at New High. 61(4):13-15 (October/December 1980)
Frequency and Duration of Disability Among Metropolitan Employees in 1977-1979. 62(1):4-6 (January/March 1981) (See also similar tables and text in 62(3):8-10 (July/September 1981)
Changes in the Age Profile of the Population. 62(3):3-4 (July/September 1981)
Long Term Cancer Survival Among Women. 62(3):13-15 (July/September 1981)
Hodgkin's Disease and Leukemia. 62(4):2-4 (October/December 1981)
Mortality in the United States, Canada, and Western Europe. 62(4):10-13 (October/December 1981)
Health of the Elderly. 63(1):3-5 (January/March 1982)

Accidents Among Women. 63(1):12-15 (January/March 1982)
Office Visits to Physicians. 63(2):5-7 (April/June 1982)
Mortality From Peptic Ulcers in the U.S. 63(2):7-9 (April/June 1982)
Geographic Variations in Mortality from Cancer. 63(3):2-6 (July/
    September 1982)
Continued Increase in Elderly Population (Including Resident
    Population at Age 65 and Over). 63(3):6-10 (July/September 1982)
Accident Mortality at the Older Ages. 63(3):10-12 (July/September 1982)
Recent Trends in Suicide. 63(4):2-4 (October/December 1982)
Characteristics of Office Visits to Physicians. 63(4):5-8 (October/
    December 1982)

Steitz, Jean A. Female Life Course: Life Situations and Perception of Control.
    INTERNATIONAL JOURNAL OF AGING AND HUMAN DEVELOPMENT. 14(3):195-205
    (1981-1982)

Forty-five males and 45 females, representing three age status periods
(adolescence, adulthood, and retired adulthood) took part in this multi-
variate cohort study. The author examined the effect of the individual's
sex and age status on the subjective perception of control and personal
efficacy in family life situations from three activity areas (home, work,
and school). Adult females perceived a greater degree of influence on
"powerful others" than adolescent or retired females, but the same as
males of any age status period. The implications of these results for the
female life course are discussed.

Stiglin, Laura E. A Classic Case of Overreaction: Women and Social Security.
    NEW ENGLAND ECONOMIC REVIEW. January/February 1981. pp. 29-40.

Although certain groups of women appear to be treated inequitably under
Social Security, in general women receive favorable treatment under the
present system. The author thinks inequities facing women will become
less serious over time, and that minor Social Security reform could reduce
these inequities.

Stoddard, Karen M. SAINTS AND SHREWS: WOMEN AND AGING IN AMERICAN POPULAR
    FILM. Westport, Connecticut, Greenwood Press, 1983. 174 pp.
    (Contributions in Women's Studies, No. 39)

The author suggests that, in trying to reach a broad paying audience,
films neglect poor and minority groups, traditionally dealing with the
middle and upper economic classes. In projecting a negative picture of
the older women, films cater to the social attitudes and myths of the
audience itself, getting into the swing of a cycle which gives an audience
what it seems to expect and then having a captive audience that accepts
what is provided. Stoddard analyzes various classes of pictures and the
women portrayed and attitudes exhibited. Specific movies are cited as
illustrations. This is a detailed treatment of older women in movies
and how they are represented or misrepresented.

Stratton, Joanna L. PIONEER WOMEN: VOICES FROM THE KANSAS FRONTIER.
    Introduction by Arthur M. Schlesinger, Jr. New York, Simon and Schuster,
    1981. 319 pp.

    Early United States counted in its population unnumbered men and women
    pioneers who underwent many hardships as they migrated West. History has
    recorded a great deal about the pioneer men, but very little of the
    pioneer women. This book corrects the record in Kansas, and is a chronicle
    from their own statements. They tell of the problems, hardships of the
    journey, settlement, social and living inadequacies, and war. These were
    not all young resilient women. Many were women of middle years, uprooted
    from comfortable existence in the East, to begin again in the Mid-West.

Streib, Gordon F. and Madeline Haug Penna. Anticipating Transitions: Possible
    Options in "Family" Forms. In: Berardo M., ed. Middle and Late Life
    Transitions. ANNALS OF THE AMERICAN ACADEMY OF POLITICAL AND SOCIAL
    SCIENCE. 464:104-119 (November 1982)

    Major trends away from the traditional family (to households of unrelated
    persons, increased single-parent families, and increased divorced persons)
    are resulting in other forms of living arrangements than those of the
    nuclear family, such as the halfway house and cooperative living. Authors
    suggest some variants of these arrangements might be adapted on an experi-
    mental basis for mid-life women who need more social supports and
    increased life-style choices. Authors discuss the current living arrange-
    ments and marital status of mid-life women; the voluntary family, why it
    is needed and what it can offer to mid-life women; and alternative living
    arrangements.

Sullivan, Deborah A. and Sylvia A. Stevens. Snowbirds: Seasonal Migrants to
    the Sunbelt. RESEARCH ON AGING. 4(2):159-177 (June 1982)

    Examines the seasonal migration of retirees to trailer and mobile home
    parks in Florida. A comparison is made of the socioeconomic and
    demographic characteristics of female participants with women of a similar
    age range in the United States, showing that the women participants are
    white, married, well-educated retirees from the north central and western
    states.

Szinovacz, Maximiliane E. Beyond the Hearth: Older Women and Retirement.
    In: Markson, Elizabeth W., ed. OLDER WOMEN: ISSUES AND PROSPECTS.
    Lexington, Massachusetts, Lexington Books, D.C. Heath & Co., 1983.
    pp. 93-120.

    Earlier research assumed that women retiring from the work force simply
    went back into the traditional occupation of housewife with no retirement
    adjustment problems. Retirement is a significant life transition not only
    for men, but also for women, although research has usually concentrated on
    men, to the exclusion of women. Persons planning retirement programs for
    women should take cognizance of their real problems. Extensive
    bibliography (8 pp.).

Szinovacz, Maximiliane. Personal Problems and Adjustment to Retirement.
    In: Szinovacz, Maximiliane, ed. WOMEN'S RETIREMENT: POLICY IMPLICATIONS
    OF RECENT RESEARCH. Beverly Hills, California, Sage Publications, 1982.
    pp. 195-203.

    Among the variables identified in earlier studies as having impact on
    older women's adjustment to retirement are: income; health; social and
    leisure activities; and attitudes toward retirement. The author attempts
    to identify relationships between a woman's perceptions of her problems
    and various indicators of retirement adjustment (the objective situational
    factors being under control). Szinovacz bases her findings on extensive
    face-to-face meetings with women who had retired within five years prior
    to the interviews. She concluded the results provided clear evidence that
    her premise was correct, that a woman's perceptions of problems play an
    important role in her adjustment to retirement.

Szinovacz, Maximiliane. Research on Women's Retirement. In: Szinovacz,
    Maximiliane, ed. WOMEN'S RETIREMENT: POLICY IMPLICATIONS OF RECENT
    RESEARCH. Beverly Hills, California, Sage Publications, 1982. pp. 13-21.

    In spite of increased interest in retirement issues in general, social
    scientists have neglected women's retirement. Szinovacz points out docu-
    mentation on the prevalent gender bias in the retirement literature and
    suggests reasons for this trend. She suggests the specific areas needing
    research in comparative and longitudinal studies in all kinds of
    employment, both blue-collar and white-collar, and especially the retire-
    ment experiences of self-employed professionals, small business and pri-
    vate service workers, and the rural population.

Szinovacz, Maximiliane. Retirement Plans and Retirement Adjustment. In:
    Szinovacz, Maximiliane, ed. WOMEN'S RETIREMENT: POLICY IMPLICATIONS OF
    RECENT RESEARCH. Beverly Hills, California, Sage Publications, 1982.
    pp. 139-150.

    There are unanswered questions in retirement planning for women: the
    necessity of the planning; the best kind of retirement planning and the
    extent to which the plans are carried out; and the effects that
    nonrealization of retirement plans have on adjustment to retirement.
    All these questions require research. In the present study, the author
    attempts to find preliminary answers to these questions. She presents
    data on women's retirement plans (including which of them are carried
    out), and the relative importance of specific retirement plans to the
    retirement adjustment of the older woman.

Szinovacz, Maximiliane. Service Needs of Women Retirees. In: Szinovacz,
    Maximiliane, ed. WOMEN'S RETIREMENT: POLICY IMPLICATIONS OF RECENT
    RESEARCH. Beverly Hills, California, Sage Publications, 1982. pp. 221-233.

    Retirement is increasingly a significant life experience for a large
    number of older women, given the increased labor force participation of
    middle-aged women and the increased length of time they now spend in gain-
    ful employment. Findings from a series of research papers (see listing of

these papers in WOMEN'S RETIREMENT: POLICY IMPLICATIONS OF RECENT RESEARCH, edited by Szinovacz, in this bibliography, all of which are annotated separately) provide ample evidence that a woman's retirement experience may differ in various ways from the retirement experience of a man. Major differences exist again in the subgroups of retired women. Szinovacz strongly recommends research on specific problems of these diverse groups of retired women, and the development of programs to help them prepare for and adapt to the retirement transition. She lists some of these problems and needs as: economic security; use of leisure time; household responsibilities and marital relations; retirement preparation; and use of and satisfaction with services available to them.

Szinovacz, Maximiliane E. WOMEN'S ADJUSTMENT TO RETIREMENT: FINAL REPORT. Tallahassee, Florida, Florida State University, Department of Sociology, March 1982. 90 pp. + bibliography (9 pp.) + 86 tables.

The major objective of this interview survey of 115 recently retired women was to obtain exploratory and in-depth information on the life situation and retirement adjustment of each woman. Major results are presented in the section on "Summary and Conclusions" under: work, retirement, social contacts, daily routines and activities, marital relations, retirement attitudes and plans, retirement problems, and retirement adjustment. The comprehensive bibliography is outstanding.

Szinovacz, Maximiliane, ed. WOMEN'S RETIREMENT: POLICY IMPLICATIONS OF RECENT RESEARCH. Beverly Hills, California, Sage Publications, 1982. 271 pp. (Sage Yearbooks in Women's Policy Studies, Vol. 6)

The editor calls this "the first book-length publication of research specifically devoted to women's retirement." There are 15 original contributions, whose primary objectives are to extend the knowledge base on this widely neglected issue and to discuss policy implications derived from this evidence. She points out the need to confirm the belief of many researchers that the retirement of women varies substantially from the retirement of men, and that these differences suggest policy implications. Contents as follows (these articles abstracted separately in this bilbiography):

Szinovacz, Maximiliane. Research on Women's Retirement. pp. 13-21.
O'Rand, Angela and John C. Henretta. Midlife Work History and Retirement Income. pp. 25-44.
Riddick, Carol Cutler. Life Satisfaction Among Aging Women: a Causal Model. pp. 45-59.
Depner, Charlene and Berit Ingersoll. Employment Status and Social Support: The Experience of the Mature Woman. pp. 61-76.
Keith, Pat M. Working Women Versus Homemakers: Retirement Resources and Correlates of Well-Being. pp. 77-91.
Kroeger, Naomi. Preretirement Preparation: Sex Differences in Access, Sources and Use. pp. 95-111.
Newman, Evelyn S., Susan R. Sherman, and Claire E. Higgins. Retirement Expectations and Plans: a Comparison of Professional Men and Women. pp. 113-122.

Price-Bonham, Sharon and Carolyn Kitchings Johnson. Attitudes Toward
    Retirement: a Comparison of Professional and Nonprofessional
    Married Women. pp. 123-138.
Szinovacz, Maximiliane. Retirement Plans and Retirement Adjustment.
    pp. 139-150.
Atchley, Robert C. The Process of Retirement: Comparing Women and
    Men. pp. 153-168.
Jewson, Ruth Hathaway. After Retirement: an Exploratory Study of
    the Professional Woman. pp. 169-182.
Block, Marilyn R. Professional Women: Work Pattern as a Correlate of
    Retirement Satisfaction. pp. 183-194.
Szinovacz, Maximiliane. Personal Problems and Adjustment to Retirement.
    pp. 195-203.
Brubaker, Timothy H. and Charles B. Hennon. Responsibility for
    Household Tasks: Comparing Dual-Earner and Dual-Retired Marriages.
    pp. 205-219.
Szinovacz, Maximiliane. Service Needs of Women Retirees. pp. 221-233.
Bibliography: pp. 235-267.

Taeuber, Cynthia M. America in Transition: an Aging Society. In: U.S.
    Congress. Senate. Special Commitee on Aging. DEVELOPMENTS IN AGING,
    1982, Vol. 1. Washington, D.C., U.S. Government Printing Office,
    1983. pp. 1-41.

    In this summary of the aging society of America, the status and problems
    of the older woman are given considerable attention throughout the
    discussion and statistical tables: demography; income and poverty; health;
    marital status; and labor force participation.

Tate, Lenore Artie. Life Satisfaction and Death Anxiety in Aged Women.
    INTERNATIONAL JOURNAL OF AGING AND HUMAN DEVELOPMENT. 15(4):299-306
    (1982-83)

    The life satisfaction and death anxiety of elderly women were investigated
    as a function of demographic, life history and stress variables.

Taylor, Sue Perkins. Mental Health and Successful Coping Among Aged Black
    Women. In: Manuel, Ron C., ed. MINORITY AGING. Westport, Connecticut,
    Greenwood Press, 1982. pp. 95-100.

    Little is known specifically about aging in black women. This article
    focuses on prevalent adjustment patterns of 84 women between the ages
    59-97 in a New England community, and draws on data collected during a
    1976-1977 ethnographic study of the lifestyle and coping strategies of
    these women. Their successful adjustment modes drew on family contacts,
    religion, their networks of friends and relatives, and, importantly,
    their lifelong attitudes toward their common cultural experiences.

Taylor, Sue Perkins. Religion as a Coping Mechanism for Older Black Women.
NCBA QUARTERLY CONTACT (National Caucus/Center on Black Aged). 5(4):2-3
(1982)

A study, completed in 1978, of 18 black women, aged 59-97, in a New England
area, shows how they used religious beliefs and practices in problem
solving. The negative aspect of what is otherwise a positive use of personal religion lies in their tendency to avoid necessary direct confron-
tation with their problems (that is, to seek formalized help with them),
thereby keeping intact their faith and ascribing the lack of solution to
"God's will."

Thompson, Gayle B. Economic Status of Late Middle-Aged Widows. In: Datan,
Nancy and Nancy Lohman, eds. TRANSITIONS OF AGING. New York, Academic
Press, 1980. pp. 133-149.

Article examined the economic status of late middle-aged widows immedi-
ately before their eligibility for Social Security benefits at age 60.
Author describes the income, labor force, and demographic characteristics
of these widows; analyzes the impact of employment on their economic status;
and, lastly, analyzes the labor force determinants of economic status among
employed widows. The data are drawn from the Retirement History Study,
beginning with initial interviews in 1969 with 11,153 individuals aged
58-63 (married and unmarried men and unmarried women) and continuing the
interviews to 1979 at 2-year intervals.

Thurmond, Gerald T. and John C. Belcher. Dimensions of Disengagement Among
Black and White Rural Elderly. INTERNATIONAL JOURNAL OF AGING AND HUMAN
DEVELOPMENT. 12(4):245-266 (1980-1981)

From a larger group of 384 persons who participated in a 1964-1965 longitudinal survey in a Georgia county on rural retirement lifestyles, those
over 55 in 1975 were selected to be re-interviewed, with varying percen-
tages of black/white males, and black/white females, to test hypothetical
disengagement theories. Those with poor health were excluded. The text
and tables present analyses by age/sex/race in such areas as: participation in formal organizations; role loss; visiting with friends; and
status of morale. The authors concede some rather puzzling conclusions,
but the central findings do indicate that this Southern rural and non-
white sample is not disengaged from social life.

Timberlake, Elizabeth M. The Value of Grandchildren to Grandmothers. JOURNAL
OF GERONTOLOGICAL SOCIAL WORK. 3(1):63-76 (Fall 1980)

The values of grandchildren to 90 grandmothers, 30 providing child care,
30 living in the same city but not providing regular child care and 30
living in different cities.

Torrey, Barbara Boyle. DEMOGRAPHIC SHIFTS AND PROJECTIONS: THE IMPLICATIONS FOR PENSION SYSTEMS. Washington, D.C., U.S. Government Printing Office, 1980. 39 pp.

Pension plans are affected by longevity of women, sex ratios, birth rates, and labor force participation of women. These aspects of the more general demographic picture are touched on briefly, with seven out of 19 tables presenting data by age/sex. This publication was issued as a "Working Paper" for the President's Commission on Pension Policy.

Treas, Judith. Aging and the Family. In: Woodruff, Diana S. and James E. Birren, eds. AGING: SCIENTIFIC PERSPECTIVES AND SOCIAL ISSUES. 2d ed. Monterey, California, Brooks/Cole Publishing Co., 1983. pp. 95-109.

In her discussion of the later family life-cycle (pp. 99-103), Treas points out that the "empty nest syndrome" which characterizes many middle-aged women is compounded by fading youth, beauty, and sex appeal. She mentions other personality characteristics of the older women. The chapter includes a small section on widowhood (pp. 103-105).

Treas, Judith and Anke Van Hilst. Marriage and Remarriage Rates Among Older Americans. In: Hendricks, Jon and C. David Hendricks, eds. DIMENSIONS OF AGING: READINGS. Cambridge, Massachusetts, Winthrop Publishers, Inc., 1979. pp. 208-213.

Based on U.S. vital statistical data for 1970, the most recent year for which detailed marriage registration figures were available to them, the authors assess the frequency of new marriages in old age, document the trends, identify those older people most likely to wed, and comment on some of the feelings and customs involved in these marriages. Men, incidentally, are six times more likely to wed in later life than women. The authors conclude that there is little reason, in the near future, to expect late-life unions to rise above their present low levels.

Treas, Judith. Women's Employment and Its Implications for the Status of the Elderly of the Future. In: Kiesler, Sara B. et al. AGING: SOCIAL CHANGE. New York, Academic Press, 1981. (Aging [Series], ed. by James G. March). pp. 561-585.

Suggests that what is most important about women's labor force participation today is its persistence and seeming inevitability, and points out that high rates of labor force participation by young women indicate that a good many women will be spending most of their lives in paid employment. The rise in female labor force participation has had an impact on Social Security. The same rise in labor force participation acts to offset the growing population of older retirees.

Troll, Lillian E. and Eugenia M. Parron. Age Changes in Sex Roles Amid Changing Sex Roles: the Double Shift. ANNUAL REVIEW OF GERONTOLOGY AND GERIATRICS, 2:118-143 (1981)

The authors discuss the current and background thinking on sex-role shifts from middle adulthood through old age (the identification of which they feel is like trying to walk through quicksand). They divide the review of the literature under four questions: 1) Are there developmental sex-role changes during adulthood? 2) Are any sex-role behaviors lost/added in later life? 3) What causes sex/role transformations in later life? and 4) What are the consequences of sex/role changes in later life? Extensive bibliography.

Troll, Lillian E. CONTINUATIONS: ADULT DEVELOPMENT AND AGING. Monterey, California, Brooks/Cole Publishing Co., 1982. 431 pp.

Text for students of the psychology of adult development and aging, covering the problems of the aging process. Contrasts men and women throughout, and relevant statistics are by sex. Chapter 13, "Work and Achievement of Women," is especially useful as so many middle-aged or older women are returning to the world of work. In the Subject Index, some headings narrow the entries to women. Bibliography: pp. 381-421.

Turner, Barbara F. The Self-Concepts of Older Women. RESEARCH ON AGING. 1(4):456-480 (1979)

By definition, "self-concept" means "how people feel about themselves in relation to others." This article reports on self-concepts of the older woman in terms of: self-esteem; internal control; age identification; and identity. It is noted that older women find increased self-esteem in terms of the more masculine-like roles, rather than feminine roles.

Turner, Barbara F. and Catherine Adams. The Sexuality of Older Women. In: Markson, Elizabeth W., ed. OLDER WOMEN: ISSUES AND PROSPECTS. Lexington, Massachusetts, Lexington Books, D.C. Heath & Co., 1983. pp. 55-72.

The particular focus in this article is on how the sexuality of women is influenced by gender (the social-psychological dimension of sex status) and by aging. Patterns of sexual behavior and attitudes about sexuality are more variable among women than among men at all ages; thus, it is very difficult to formulate general statements about the sexuality of older women. Primary emphasis in this article is on the aging process, which includes changes in sexual physiology and health, and on generational or historical shifts over time in sexual attitudes and practices. Gender differences are discussed throughout.

Uhlenberg, Peter and Mary Anne P. Myers. Divorce and the Elderly. GERONTOLO-GIST. 21(3):276-282 (June 1981)

Discusses the level of divorce among the elderly, how it is likely to change in the future, and the implications of these changes. The tables are by sex.

Uhlenberg, Peter. Older Women: The Growing Challenge to Design Constructive Roles. GERONTOLOGIST. 19(3):236-241 (June 1979)

A study of the years 1970 to 2000, examining the characteristics of successive cohorts of old women and the social structure of the old-age stage of life as it currently exists. The well-being and independence of the older woman are enhanced by her participation in socially acceptable roles.

U.S. Bureau of Labor Statistics. EMPLOYMENT IN PERSPECTIVE: WORKING WOMEN, ANNUAL SUMMARY, 1982. Washington, D.C., 1982. 3 pp. (Report 677)

The significant data on women in the civilian labor force in 1982 include several tables in which women over 55 are indicated: labor force participation; employment status; and unemployment rates. Other statistics are for the total labor force of women over 16, as is most of the text.

U.S. Bureau of the Census. American Families and Living Arrangements. CURRENT POPULATION REPORTS, SERIES P-23, No. 104, May 1980. 18 pp.

A number of tables present information by sex/age for: decline in marriage; ratio of divorced/married; persons living alone; and median age of mothers at death of spouse (1880-1970s).

U.S. Bureau of the Census. Estimates of the Population of the United States, by Age, Sex, and Race: 1980 to 1982. CURRENT POPULATION REPORTS, SERIES P-25, No. 929, May 1983. 25 pp.

Estimates of the total population (including Armed Forces overseas); of the resident population; and of the civilian population, all by age, sex, and race, July 1, 1980 to 1982. A fourth table gives population by type, age, sex, and Office of Management and Budget-consistent race, April 1, 1980.

U.S. Bureau of the Census. Illustrated Projctions of State Population by Age, Race, and Sex: 1975 to 2000. CURRENT POPULATION REPORTS, SERIES P-25, No. 796, 1979. 164 pp.

Projections of the total population by states, in five-year increments, by race/sex/age. In addition, four of the eight tables in the appendix give estmates by race/sex/age outmigration and inmigration by state.

U.S. Bureau of the Census. Social and Economic Characteristics of the Older Population: 1978. CURRENT POPULATION REPORTS, SERIES P-23, No. 75, August 1979. 44 pp.

Some 20 of the tables present statistics by sex for the 55+ and 65+ population (black, white, Spanish-speaking origin) on: marital and family status; institutional population; nativity and parentage; mobility and residence; voting and registration; labor force, employment, occupation; income and earnings; poverty; and health and health services.

U.S. Bureau of the Census. Social and Economic Status of the Black Population
in the United States: an Historical View, 1790-1978. CURRENT POPULATION
REPORTS, SERIES P-23, No. 80, June 1979. 271 pp.

Various tables and some text throughout present information by age/sex on
changes which have occurred in population distribution, income levels,
mortality, education, employment, family composition, and other major
aspects of the life of blacks, assembling in one report data published
previously in many different sources. The historical trends (1790-1975)
and the recent trends (1975-1978) are presented separately.

U.S. Bureau of the Census. Statistical Portrait of Women in the United States:
1978. CURRENT POPULATION REPORTS, SERIES P-23, No. 100, February 1983.
169 pp.

A statistical overview of the changing status of women in American society
during the 1970 decade, with data compiled primarily from U.S. government
sources, assembled here to document the patterns of demographic, social
and economic change that have affected American women in the 1970's.
Supporting the text are age/sex tables and figures on: population growth
and distribution; longevity, mortality, and health; labor force participation; work experience; income and poverty status; crime victims; and
special sections on black women, American Indian women, Asian women, and
Spanish-origin women. Appendix of base tables.

U.S. Congress. Congressional Budget Office. WORK AND RETIREMENT: OPTIONS FOR
CONTINUED EMPLOYMENT OF OLDER WORKERS. Washington, D.C., U.S. Government
Printing Office, July 1982. 63 pp.

Tables 1-4 are by sex; otherwise most of the text makes no distinction,
with the exception of widows' resources, in the discussion of Social
Security.

U.S. Congress. House. Select Committee on Aging. IMPACT OF REAGAN ECONOMICS ON
AGING WOMEN. Washington, D.C., U.S. Government Printing Office, 1983.
65 pp.

These hearings before the Subcommittee on Retirement Income and Employment, in Portland, Oregon, September 1982, were conducted in four panels,
each with several leading specialists as witnesses: 1) Social Security
and income maintenance (including Elizabeth Meyer and Jean Bader); 2) Impact
of health care cuts on older women (Jane Gleason); 3) Impact of budget
cuts on community service programs for the elderly (Nancy Russel-Young);
4) Impact of Reagan budget cuts on older women (Woodrow Wilson and Nora
Kenhoff).

U.S. Congress. House. Select Committee on Aging. NATIONAL POLICY PROPOSALS
AFFECTING MIDLIFE WOMEN: HEARINGS BEFORE THE SUBCOMMITTEE ON RETIREMENT
INCOME AND EMPLOYMENT. Washington, D.C., U.S. Government Printing Office,
1979. 284 pp.

These hearings, in May 1979, presented 29 distinguished and knowledgeable
persons and organizations as witnesses for action on a national policy

now on the 26 million midlife women of today (between 40 and 60) who are going to be our 65+ female population some years hence.

U.S. Congress. House. Select Committee on Aging. PROBLEMS OF AGING WOMEN: HEARING, OMAHA, NEBRASKA, July 26, 1982. Washington, D.C., U.S. Government Printing Office, 1982. 157 pp.

The speakers, witnesses and service providers, addressed the concerns of aging women of Nebraska, concerns which were not necessarily just local. They touched on economic well-being, employment, retirement income, Social Security, services and programs, health care, spouse loss, etc. Representative Daub (of Nebraska) pointed out that, although the programs were not specifically set up for women, nevertheless women are indeed the major participants of the programs on aging.

U.S. Congress. House. Select Committee on Aging. TREATMENT OF WOMEN UNDER SOCIAL SECURITY. Washington, D.C., U.S. Government Printing Office, 1980-1981. 3 vols. (331 + 494 + 206 pp.)

Volumes 1 and 3 of these hearings before the Task Force on Social Security and Women, of the Subcommittee on Retirement Income and Employment, contain the presentations of experts on the inequities in the Social Security system for older women. Vol. 2, additionally, contains various proposals concerning Social Security and women, and several full-length reprinted papers (two of which are abstracted separately in this bibliography): U.S. Department of Health, Education and Welfare, "Social Security and the Changing Roles of Men and Women," and another title from HEW, "Report of the HEW Task Force on the Treatment of Women Under Social Security." Two full-length papers in Vol. 3 (likewise abstracted separately in this bibliography) are: O'Farrell, Brendan, "Pensions and Divorce," and Lapkoff, Shelley, "Working Women, Marriage, and Retirement."

U.S. Congress. House. Select Committee on Aging. WOMEN AND RETIREMENT INCOME PROGRAMS: CURRENT ISSUES OF EQUITY AND ADEQUACY. Washington, D.C., U.S. Government Printing Office, 1979. 119 pp.

This report was prepared by the Congressional Research Service of the Library of Congress for the Select Committee's Subcommittee on Retirement Income and Employment. Income to support retired workers and their dependents and survivors comes from a number of separate public and private programs and systems. Due to changes in work patterns and family living arrangements, serious questions now raise themselves concerning the equity and adequacy of such retirement income benefits to women. Although most so-called inequities and inadequacies do not result from overt program discrimination against women, changes are possible which would make programs respond better to women's changing roles and requirements.

U.S. Congress. House. Select Committee on Aging. WOMEN IN MIDLIFE: SECURITY AND FULFILLMENT: A COMPENDIUM OF PAPERS, Vol. 2. Washington, D.C., U.S. Government Printing Office, 1979. 181 pp.

The second volume of this two-volume compendium of papers for the Subcommittee on Retirement Income and Employment was prepared by the

Library of Congress Congressional Research Service and lists works
(many annotated) in subject groupings: Perspective; The Challenge of Change;
The World of Work and Education; Money Matters; Special Needs and Supports;
Leadership; and Conclusion (Prospects for Middle-Aged Women). The
material is mostly drawn from 1975-1978 imprints and constitutes a careful
combing of the resources of the Library of Congress. Vol. 1, released in
1978, consists of about 20 original papers by well-known specialists.

U.S. Department of Health, Education, and Welfare. Report of the HEW Task
    Force on the Treatment of Women Under Social Security. In: U.S. Congress.
    House. Select Committee on Aging. TREATMENT OF WOMEN UNDER SOCIAL
    SECURITY, Vol. 2. Washington, D.C., U.S. Government Printing Office, 1980.
    pp. 348-377.

    While the Social Security program since its enactment more than 40 years
    ago has expanded and changed considerably, the basic unit for providing
    family protection still remains the married couple consisting of a life-
    long paid worker and a lifelong unpaid homemaker. But the changing social
    trend is to changing work roles within families; changing perceptions of
    other roles within families; and increasing rates of marital dissolution.
    Reviews suggestions for changing the benefit structure so as to accommodate
    the increasing diversity of these family patterns, all of which address
    the issues of fairness at retirement, take account of the earnings of
    both spouses in two-earner couples, and provide equal or more nearly
    equal benefits for one- and two-earner couples with the same average life-
    time earnings credits. None of these plans resolves broader issues
    about gaps in protection, inadequate benefits, or overlapping credits for
    homemakers who become disabled, divorced, or widowed before retirement.
    Some plans even raise new problems. The Task Force concluded that provi-
    sions for family protection and the treatment of women under Social
    Security require further attention by HEW so that policymakers and the
    public may have clear choices about alternative forms of protection under
    Social Security.

U.S. Department of Health, Education, and Welfare. SOCIAL SECURITY AND THE
    CHANGING ROLES OF MEN AND WOMEN. Washington, D.C., February 1979.
    323 pp.

    Report mandated by Congress under P.L. 95-216 to "study proposals to
    eliminate dependency as a factor in entitlement to spouse's benefits and
    to eliminate sex discrimination under the Social Security program." Ch. 1
    reviews present and past provisions of the law as a basis for analyzing
    and evaluating options for a changed program. The issues mainly center
    around the fact that most married women have Social Security protection as
    their husbands' dependents, but cannot receive both those benefits and
    those they may also be entitled to from their own work earnings. Various
    concerns as to adequacy and equity are the result. The succeeding chap-
    ters consider the options (comprehensive and limited) and gender-based
    distinctions. The appendices present interesting collateral materials.

U.S. Department of State. U.S. NATIONAL REPORT ON AGING FOR THE UNITED NATIONS WORLD ASSEMBLY ON AGING. Washington, D.C., Government Printing Office, June 1982. 133 pp.

"Demographic Trends and Projections" (pp. 12-25) presents five out of 11 tables by sex/age. A paragraph in "Issues" (p. 25) notes that a pronounced imbalance between the sexes among older age groups will persist, suggesting that most of our social programs must be geared to the needs of older women. In the chapter on "Employment and Retirement," the labor force participation is projected to the year 2000, by age/sex, with the comment that the increase of women's participation is significant and that any growth in older workers which occurs in the next two decades will be greatly influenced by the decisions of women to remain in the labor force.

U.S. General Accounting Office. DEMOGRAPHIC AND ECONOMIC CHARACTERISTICS OF SOCIAL SECURITY RETIREE FAMILIES. Washington, D.C., September 1982. 61 pp.

Interesting tables with brief statements, some of which relate directly to wives who benefit through their husbands' Social Security payments. See Table 3 (Awards to Wives and Husbands of Retirees, 1965, 1970, and 1975-1979); Tables 5-6 (Entitlement Benefits by Wife and Husband, in 1978, and 1968-1978); Table 9 (Changes in Benefit Awards, 1975-1979, to Wives, by Age). Remaining tables describe beneficiaries in other general terms.

U.S. Government Printing Office. SUBJECT BIBLIOGRAPHY [on] WOMEN. Washington, D.C., November 5, 1982. 17 pp.

This general bibliography on women includes dozens of references to publications, obtainable from the Superintendent of Documents, which concern the older woman: displaced homemaker (and her legal status, state by state); employment; education; retirement; Social Security; and issues and policies.

U.S. National Center for Health Statistics. Advance Report of Final Mortality Statistics, 1979. MONTHLY VITAL STATISTICS REPORT. 31(6, Supplement), September 30, 1982. 59 pp.

Death rates by age, race, and sex; life expectancy; leading causes of death (diseases, accidents, etc.); and place of death, are among the tables in which statistics are by sex and age.

U.S. National Center for Health Statistics. Annual Summary of Births, Deaths, Marriages, and Divorces: United States, 1981. MONTHLY VITAL STATISTICS REPORT. 30(13), December 20, 1982. 27 pp.

Tables 5 and 6 present death rates by age, race, and sex (Table 6 for 1981 alone) in 10-year age groups, for 1950, 1960, and from 1971 year by year through 1981.

U.S. National Center for Health Statistics. Basic Data on Health Care Needs of Adults, Aged 25-74 Years, United States, 1971-1975. VITAL AND HEALTH STATISTICS, SERIES 11, No. 218, 1980. 45 pp.

Report presents national estimates of selected health care needs of adults by age, race, sex, and family income group, derived from the first National Health and Nutrition Examination Survey, conducted between April 1971 and October 1975.

U.S. National Center for Health Statistics. HEALTH, UNITED STATES, 1980. Washington, D.C., U.S. Government Printing Office, December 1980. 323 pp.

In this survey of health in the U.S., 12 of the 78 detailed tables for 1980 give statistics by age and sex on death rates; life expectancy at birth; mortality (heart diseases and cancer); cigarette smokers; non-federal hospital stays; and nursing home residents.

U.S. National Center for Health Statistics. HEALTH, UNITED STATES, 1982. Washington, D.C., U.S. Government Printing Office, December 1982. 191 pp.

In this 1982 survey of health in the United States, emphasizing trends and comparisons over time, Part A consists of text and 16 charts on health status and determinants organized by age from the youngest group to the oldest, and in pp. 28-37, treats of the middle-aged and elderly, and touches on sex differences. In Part B, out of the 86 detailed tables, 13 give statistics by age and sex on: mortality from various diseases; suicide and homicide; cigarette smokers; hospital stays; and nursing home residents. Death rates for all causes by race, sex and age from 1950-1980 are given on pp. 51-52.

U.S. National Commission for Employment Policy. INCREASING THE EARNINGS OF DISADVANTAGED WOMEN. Washington, D.C., U.S. Government Printing Office, January 1981. 171 pp.

This Commission examined the economic situation of disadvantaged women (women divorced or re-entering the labor market after their child rearing years), sponsored two conferences and several research efforts (see Appendix B), and made 20 policy recommendations for improving earnings. Basic to these recommendations is partnership by the Federal, state, and local governments and by the private sector.

U.S. National Commission on Social Security. SOCIAL SECURITY IN AMERICA'S FUTURE: FINAL REPORT, MARCH 1981. Washington, D.C., U.S. Government Printing Office, 1981. 414 pp.

In this Final Report, the Commission addresses itself specifically to women in Ch. 11, "Women and Social Security." Other chapters occasionally differentiate between men and women as to their Social Security status and benefits. The National Commission states that it has been particularly concerned about the adequacy and the equity of protection accorded to women under the Social Security program, and it recommends two changes be made, and a third given serious consideration.

1) Raise the maximum amount of the special minimum benefit that Social Security pays to people who have had long working careers at low wages.

2) Improve benefits for aged widows whose husbands die long before retirement age.

3) Make some change in the impact of divorce on the availability of Social Security benefits for women.

The Commission defends the overall interest of Social Security in women, but concedes that certain subgroups have insufficient and/or inequitable protection under Social Security.

U.S. National Commission on Social Security Reform. REPORT OF THE COMMISSION. Washington, D.C., U.S. Government Printing Office, January 1983. Sections repaged.

The National Commission reviewed the results of the many hearings, studies, and reports of other public bodies, including Congress, the 1979 Advisory Council on Social Security, and the 1981 National Commission on Social Security. In Ch. 2 (Major Findings and Recommendations of the Commission), Recommendation No. 9 deals specifically with changes and benefit provisions which would mainly affect women. Some of the supplementary statements by individual members of the Commission likewise mention special needs of women, as in that by Robert M. Ball (and others selected by the Democratic leadership of Congress) in a three-page statement on meeting problems of special concern to women.

U.S. National Institute on Aging. THE OLDER WOMAN: CONTINUITIES AND DISCONTINUITIES: REPORT OF THE NATIONAL INSTITUTE ON AGING AND THE NATIONAL INSTITUTE OF MENTAL HEALTH WORKSHOP, SEPTEMBER 14-16, 1978. Washington, D.C., U.S. Government Printing Office, 1979. 51 pp.

Major sources of continuity throughout a woman's life are her "kinkeeper" function (her emotional relationships with parents, siblings, offspring, friends), and her housekeeper activities. The discontinuities include intermittent labor force participation, marriage, divorce, geographic mobility, and income (often related to her marital status or changes in the husband's employment). The conference focused on these contrasting sides of a woman's life, stressing the heterogeneity among older women. It agreed that data to understand the lives and needs of older women are not available in many areas: data other than women as wives, mothers or heads of households; longitudinal data on their labor force participation; family life and networks; longevity of women; and information on minority women. The conference agreed that research should be based on relevant social, economic and political events of the times, with cross-cultural perspectives through historical and anthropological research.

U.S. National Institute on Aging. SPECIAL REPORT ON AGING, 1982. Bethesda, Maryland, September 1982. 24 pp.

Latest in a series of annual reports on its continued exploration of a wide range of medical and psychosocial issues affecting the nation's growing older population. In the following areas, as reported on in this annual report, research was by sex; body composition baselines established for healthy people at different ages; K. Warner Schaie's research on whether intelligence can improve with age; effect of death of spouse on longevity; and women's retirement decisions.

U.S. President's Advisory Committee for Women. VOICES FOR WOMEN. Washington, D.C., 1980. 192 pp.

Four of the chapters in this ninth report to the President on the status of women in the U.S. cover the most critical issues in broad areas: health; human services; work and income security; and education; with overviews and comments of the Commission. Although the issue of older women is touched on briefly in every area, the only substantive subsection (in Ch. 4 on Health) is that on "Older Women" (pp. 61-63), where the question was how to improve the quality of the lives we are now prolonging. The PACFW recommendation is that Title 20 of the Social Security Act should be expanded for homemaker services, home management services, and home health services for older women.

U.S. Social Security Administration. A WOMAN'S GUIDE TO SOCIAL SECURITY. Washington, D.C., U.S. Government Printing Office, May 1982. 15 pp.

This pamphlet states very simply the terms of the Social Security Law, up to 1982, as it affects all women: wives; women with or without children; widows; and medical provisions affecting them. It is brief and understandable.

U.S. Women's Bureau. SELECTED SOURCES OF EMPLOYMENT INFORMATION FOR RE-ENTRY AND MATURE WOMEN. Washington, D.C., [1982?]. 7 pp.

A list of public and private agencies which, as of August 1982, could be helpful to women seeking to enter or re-enter the labor force.

U.S. Women's Bureau. SUMMARY AND ANALYSIS OF THE JOB TRAINING PARTNERSHIP ACT OF 1982 WITH SELECTED PROVISIONS OF INTEREST TO INDIVIDUALS AND GROUPS CONCERNED ABOUT EMPLOYMENT AND TRAINING OPPORTUNITIES FOR WOMEN. Washington, D.C., U.S. Government Printing Office, November 1982. 15 pp.

The Job Training Partnership Act of 1982 (JTPA, Public Law 97-300), replacing CETA (Comprehensive Employment and Training Act), is concerned with the needs of women, and increases to a major degree the sharing of the training for entry or re-entry of disadvantaged individuals, especially older women, back into the labor force among Federal, state and local governments, and the private sector. Part B of Title I concerns individuals economically disadvantaged and over age 55. The Act was to be fully effective October 1, 1983.

University Microfilms International. CURRENT RESEARCH ON GERONTOLOGY: A CATALOG
OF DOCTORAL DISSERTATIONS. Ann Arbor, Michigan, March 1982. 21 pp.

This catalog, in general, shows the accelerating interest in the academic
world in doctoral research in gerontology. Every section of this detailed
subject listing of dissertations includes one or several titles on the older
woman. In all, there are almost 60 dissertations on women, out of the
total 495 titles. Abstracts are to be found in DISSERTATION ABSTRACTS
INTERNATIONAL, SECTION A, HUMANITIES AND SOCIAL SCIENCES, a reference tool
found in large or research libraries.

Verbrugge, Lois M. Women and Men: Mortality and Health of Older People.
In: Hess, Beth B. and Kathleen Bond, eds. LEADING EDGES: RECENT RESEARCH
ON PSYCHOLOGICAL AGING. Washington, D.C., U.S. Government Printing
Office, 1981. pp. 231-285.

This paper is one of a series prepared for the 1981 White House Conference
on Aging by the National Institute on Aging. It reviews data on health
and mortality of older men and women and suggests reasons for the sex
differences. The paper is organized in seven sections: population data
for older men and women; past, current, and projected mortality for men
and women; contemporary sex differentials in the physical health status of
older people; differences in older people's use of health services and
drugs (medication); plausible explanations for the sex differences in
health and mortality; key research questions for testing the explanations;
and thoughts about future sex differences in health and mortality of older
people. It focuses on physical health and on psychosocial factors to
explain sex differences. Extensive references, pp. 277-285. This paper
is reprinted in: Riley, Matilda White, Beth B. Hess and Kathleen Bond,
eds., AGING IN SOCIETY: SELECTED REVIEWS OF RECENT RESEARCH. Hillsdale,
New Jersey, Lawrence Erlbaum Associates, Publishers, 1983. pp. 139-174.

Vitaliano, Peter Paul, et al. Dementia and Other Competing Risks for Mortality
in the Institutionalized Aged. JOURNAL OF THE AMERICAN GERIATRICS
SOCIETY. 29(11):513-519 (November 1981)

Relative importance of dementia, gender, age, and functional status was
examined for relationships to mortality within five years after admission
of the subjects to a nursing home for the aged. The three tables are by
sex. Authors concluded that the life-shortening effect of dementia is
similar for males and females.

Ward, Russell A. The Never-Married in Later Life. JOURNAL OF GERONTOLOGY.
34(6):861-869 (November 1979)

Analysis of the singlehood of 162 never-married persons aged 50 and over,
based on data from six years of a survey by the National Opinion Research
Center (University of Chicago). Highly educated older women were found
most likely to remain unmarried. These never-married women were less
happy in later life than the married, and only slightly happier than the
widowed or divorced, their unhappiness apparently resulting from greater
dissatisfaction with the type of family life of which they formed a part.

Warlick, Jennifer L.   Aged Women in Poverty: a Problem Without a Solution?
    In: Browne, William P. and Laura Katz Olson, eds.   AGING AND PUBLIC
    POLICY: THE POLITICS OF GROWING OLD IN AMERICA.   Westport, Connecticut,
    Greenwood Press, 1983.   pp. 35-66.

    Aged females are twice as likely as their male counterparts to have total
    cash income below the poverty line.   Only when race is introduced is there
    a subgroup of males with a higher incidence of poverty than females.   The
    explanation of why this difference exists includes examining the sex dif-
    ferentials in both pre-transfer income and pre-transfer poverty; the
    sporadic work histories of the worker/homemaker and her concentration in
    jobs not covered by private pension plans; and differentiation of Social
    Security between beneficiaries on the basis of marital status favoring
    married couples.   The future aspect of the dilemma depends on trends in
    the labor force; pension plans and retirement systems; Social Security
    reform; and marital, age, and race composition of the population of aged
    women.   Author concludes, regretfully, that dramatic improvement in the
    economic status of older women is not likely to take place in the fore-
    seeable future.

Webb, Wilse B.   Sleep in Older Persons: Sleep Stuctures of 50- to 60-Year-Old
    Men and Women.   JOURNAL OF GERONTOLOGY.   37(5):581-586, September 1982.

    Sleep measurements by electroencephalograph of equal numbers of men and
    women aged 50-60, healthy and actively employed.   The noticeable difference
    between them and younger groups of men and women is in the increased
    number and longer duration of awakenings during the night.   In addition,
    the sleep of older men is more disturbed than that of older women, men
    suffering more awakenings.   Other sex differences in sleep patterns are
    pointed out.

Weinstein, Claire E., et al.   Memory Strategies Reported by Older Adults for
    Experimental and Everyday Learning Tasks.   EDUCATIONAL GERONTOLOGY.
    7(2/3):205-213 (September/October 1981)

    Attempt to identify the types of memory strategies used by a group of
    noninstitutionalized elderly individuals, ranging in age from 60 to 96.
    Since the group of 35 persons included 31 women, the results justifiably
    apply to the older woman.

Wharton, George F.   SEXUALITY AND AGING: AN ANNOTATED BIBLIOGRAPHY.   Metuchen,
    New Jersey, Scarecrow Press, Inc., 1981.   251 pp.

    More than 1100 references presented in subject groups.   On the subject
    of "Sexuality and the Aging Female" (pp. 60-75) there are 82 annotated
    titles.

Wheeler, Helen R.   Middle-Aged "Older Woman": A Feminist Librarian's Approach to
    Library Resources.   COLLECTION BUILDING: STUDIES IN THE DEVELOPMENT AND
    EFFECTIVE USE OF LIBRARY RESOURCES.   3(1):20-30 (1981)

After an introductory treatment of the dilemma of the middle-aged woman with respect to the new challenges facing her at that age, the author presents a compilation of resource materials particularly useful to library collections serving clients directly, not through women's studies programs. The materials are divided into: bibliographies and guides to the literature; indexes and abstracts; trade books and classics; non-print materials; "alternative" publications; government sources; and a "checklist" of 38 titles, some of them from unusual sources.

White House Conference on Aging, 1981. CHARTBOOK ON AGING IN AMERICA. Compiled by Carole Allan and Herman Brotman. Washington, D.C., 1981. 141 pp.

Prepared for participants in the 1981 WHCOA, this multi-colored chartbook illustrates demograhic, economic and other developments, past, present and projected. Each page of text accompanied by charts and graphs. Material arranged in seven categories with frequent attention to problems and needs of women.

Wilkinson, Carrol Wetzel, Graham D. Rowles and Betty Maxwell. AGING IN RURAL AMERICA: A COMPREHENSIVE ANNOTATED BIBLIOGRAPHY, 1975-1981. Morgantown, Gerontology Center, West Virginia University, 1982. 119 pp.

In the subject arranged part of this bibliography, under the headings "Widows" and "Women" there are altogether 12 items on the older woman in rural America.

Willemsen, Eleanor Walker. Terman's Gifted Women: Work and the Way They See Their Lives. In: Back, Kurt W., ed. LIFE COURSE: INTEGRATIVE THEORIES AND EXEMPLARY POPULATIONS. Boulder, Colorado, Westview Press, published for the American Association for the Advancement of Science, 1980. pp. 121-132.

In 1922, Lewis Terman began his now well-known study of gifted children. The present paper is concerned with the women in Terman's gifted group and their subjective perceptions in 1977 of what events or choices have been important in their lives and how these elements have come to be influential. These gifted women are from a generation where working outside the home was definitely not the expected pattern. Many of them nevertheless worked for substantial portions of their lives though often at traditionally feminine occupations (education, librarianship, nursing). As a whole, the findings of the study show that the experience of work had a positive impact on these Terman women who worked. What the Terman women's gifts may have provided them is a capacity for experiencing accomplishment and satisfaction in the choices which they made without a lessening of self-esteem which less gifted working women might have experienced.

Williams, Blanch Spruiel. CHARACTERISTICS OF THE BLACK ELDERLY. Washington, D.C., National Clearinghouse on Aging, April 1980. 41 pp. (Statistical Reports on Older Americans, No. 5)

This statistical report examines the socio-economic and demograhic characteristics of the black elderly population. Two out of the 11 text tables and six out of the 20 detailed tables are by sex.

Williamson, John B., Linda Evans and Anne Munley. AGING AND SOCIETY. New York, Holt, Rinehart & Winston, 1980. 450 pp.

This text, intended for use in a multidisciplinary course in social gerontology, is divided into three parts: 1) the process of aging; 2) the experience of being old; and 3) the experience of dying and the process of bereavement. Ch. 3, "Sexuality," on sexuality and the older person, emphasizes the normality of the continuing sexual life after age 65. Ch. 5, "Marriage, Family and Friendship," brings up the special problems and adjustments on the part of the older woman in the husband/wife relationship (sex roles and marriage), retirement life, and widowhood. Ch. 15, "Grief, Mourning, and Widowhood," discusses the adjustment to bereavement (usually the loss of the spouse) and how women differ from men in their reactions.

Williamson, John B., Linda Evans and Lawrence A. Powell. POLITICS OF AGING: POWER AND POLICY. Springfield, Illinois, Charles C. Thomas, Publisher, 1982. 331 pp.

Issues of political gerontology are identified, analyzed and explained in this monograph. In Ch. 2, "The Aged Preindustrial Societies," the social role and varying power status of the older women are sketchily described, according to historical eras and geographical locations. Given the sparsity of such information, this small amount is welcome.

Willing,, Jules Z. REALITY OF RETIREMENT: THE INNER EXPERIENCE OF BECOMING A RETIRED PERSON. New York, William Morrow & Co., Inc., 1981. 227 pp.

Retirement involves change. This book gives much attention to the effect upon women of the changes in a man's life, especially his retirement. For example, see Ch. 3, "Impact on the Marriage Partner."

Wilson, Molly M. Enhancing the Lives of the Aged in a Retirement Center Through a Program of Reading. EDUCATIONAL GERONTOLOGY. 4(3):245-251 (1979)

Description of a reading/discussion group of representative elderly women (age 59-75) in a senior center in Athens, Georgia. The meetings were not meant to be of a therapeutic nature, but rather to promote social contacts beyond those in their otherwise somewhat meager social lives.

Winogrond, Iris Ruther. A Comparison of Interpersonal Distancing Behavior in Young and Elderly Adults. INTERNATIONAL JOURNAL OF AGING AND HUMAN DEVELOPMENT. 13(1):53-60 (1981)

Purpose of the research was to investigate the relationship between age, race, cortical activation (arousal), and interpersonal distancing behaviors in a group consisting of 18 each of: young white women; elderly white women; and elderly black women. The findings suggest that interpersonal distancing behaviors may be influenced more by the prevalence of cultural norms than by other factors.

Withers, William. THE CRISIS IN OLD AGE FINANCE. Woodbury, New York, Barron's, 1979. 293 pp.

Economic problems of the elderly and the failure of both government and private pension systems to meet the average older person's needs. Much attention to females, and many tables by sex.

Wolleat, Patricia L. Counseling the Elderly Woman: a Sex-Role Perspective. In: Pulvino, Charles J. and Nicholas Colangelo, eds. COUNSELING FOR THE GROWING YEARS: 65 AND OVER. Minneapolis, Minnesota, Educational Media Corporation, 1980. pp. 185-196.

Stresses that women are not simply growing old, but rather that they are "growing." The author addresses their disadvantaged position in society as victims of both ageism and sexism, and finishes with guidelines to counselors working with older women.

Working Women (National Association of Office Workers). VANISHED DREAMS: AGE DISCRIMINATION AND THE OLDER WOMAN WORKER. Cleveland, Ohio, August 1980. 31 pp.

Despite the important role they occupy in the U.S. economy, the more than 40 million women workers over 40 face discrimination which favors the younger woman in hiring, promotion, and salary. Theirs is the lowest median income of any wage or sex group and, regardless of their importance in the labor force, they are the fastest growing segment of the nation's poor.

World Assembly on Aging, Vienna, 1982. REPORT OF THE WORLD ASSEMBLY ON AGING. New York, United Nations, 1982. 101 pp. (A/CONF. 113/31)

In the summary of the general debate (pp. 14-35), occasional mention is made of the older woman as a special, increasing segment of the aging population of the world; her poverty; her life expectancy. In its "International Plan of Action on Aging and Other Resolutions and Decision of the World Assembly" (pp. 46-85), the status and plight of the older woman are cited several times among the pervading problems of the general population of older persons of the world.

Zimmeth, Mary. WOMEN'S GUIDE TO RE-ENTRY EMPLOYMENT. New York, Charles Scribner's Sons, 1981. 165 pp.

The number of women in the U.S., especially middle-aged and older women, who seek to enter or re-enter paid employment for greater economic security, is constantly increasing. This slim volume alerts the woman to the planning needed for the new pattern of living, and the principal means of achieving it.

Zube, Margaret. Outlook on Being Old: Working Class Elderly in Northampton, Massachusetts. GERONTOLOGIST. 20(4):427-431 (August 1980)

Study of working-class elderly in two age-segregated public housing projects (26 men and 117 women), to learn more about the importance of cultural milieu, past experiences, and environments of the aging as they relate to social behavior and philosophies of the elderly. The preponderance of women among the participants and the nature of the statements made by the participants suggest that the attitudes and philosophies expressed are women's. The author concludes that these elderly are resilient and rather secure of their image, tending to retain their earlier behavior patterns and basic orientations.

SUBJECT INDEX

ATTITUDES--SEXUALITY

  King, N.R. (Sexuality)

ATTITUDES--TIME

  Cooper, P.E.

ATTITUDES--WIVES

  Statham, A.

ATTITUDES--WOMEN

  Block, M.R. (Women)
  Aging Awareness
  Cool, L.
  Fuller, M.M.
  Gerbner, G.
  Hollenshead, C.
  Ohio State Univ.
  Shaw, L.B. (Unplanned)
  Sommers, T. (Epilogue)
  "   "   (Older Women & Health)
  Stoddard, K.M.
  Szinovacz, M. (Personal)
  "   "   (Research)

ATTITUDES--WORK

  Rosen, E.

BATTERED WOMEN

  Gesino, J.P.
  Silverman, P.R.

BIBLIOGRAPHY

  Aging Awareness
  Atchley, R.C. (Social)
  Block, M.R. (Health)
  "   "   (Women)
  Borenstein, A.
  Braito, R.
  Butler, F.R.
  Cameron, C.
  Cauhape, E.
  Cohler, B.J. (Mothers)
  Cuellar, J.B.
  Davis, L.G.
  Dement, W.C.
  Edwards, W.M.
  Employee Benefit Research Inst.
  Fuller, M.M.
  Gibson, R.C. (Work)
  Grady, S.C.

Gratton, B. (Decision)
Hess, B.B. (Family)
Jackson, J.J.
Kahne, H. (Economic Security)
King, N.R. (Issues)
Lopata, H.Z. (Economics)
"   "   (Women as)
Lowenthal, M.F.
Matthews, S.H.
Miller, D.B.
Mueller, J.E.
Nathanson, C.A.
National Retired Teachers Assoc.
Nudel, A.
O'Neill, J.A. (Male-Female)
Pellegrino, V.Y.
Porcino, J.
Rubin, L.B.
Segalla, R.A.
Seltzer, M.M.
Shock, N.W. (Current)
Szinovacz, M. (Beyond)
"   "   (Women's Adjustment)
"   "   (Women's Retirement)
Troll, L.E. (Age)
"   "   (Continuations)
U.S. Cong. House. Select Comm. on
  Aging   (Women in Midlife)
U.S. Govt. Print. Off.
University Microfilms International
Verbrugge, L.M.
Wharton, G.F.
Wheeler, H.R.
Wilkinson, C.W.

BLACKS

  Block, M.R. (Women)
  Braito, R.
  Butler, F.R.
  Chirikos, T.N. (Economic)
  "   "   (Sex)
  Cuellar, J.B.
  Davis, L.G.
  Gibson, R.C. (Race)
  "   "   (Work)
  Jackson, J.J.
  Lesnoff-Caravaglia, G. (Black)
  Lopata, H.Z. (Changing)
  Mindel, C.H.
  Nestel, G.
  North American Regional Technical
    Meeting on Aging
  Ohio State Univ.
  Quinn, J.F.
  Scott, J.P.
  Sommers, T. (Women & Aging)

Taylor, S.P. (Mental)
"   "   (Religion)
Thurmond, G.T.
U.S. Bureau of the
  Census   (Estimates)
"   "   (Social & Economic
                 Characteristics)
"   "   (Social & Economic
                 Status)
"   "   (Statistical)
William, B.S.

BUDGETS, OFFICIAL

Coalition on Women & the Budget
U.S. Cong. House. Select Comm.
  on Aging (Impact)

CAREERS

Brown, E.T.
Butler, R.N.
Catalyst
Doss, M.M.
Miller, D.B.
Rubin, L.B.
Segalla, R.A.
Sheehy, G.
Shields, L.
Zimmeth, M.

CAREGIVERS

Archbold, P.G.
Brody, E.M.
Cicirelli, V.G.
Colman, V.
Crossman, L.
Fengler, A.P. (Wives)
Hess, B.B. (Family)
Marshall, V.W.
N.Y. (State) Office for the Aging
Shanas, E.
Soldo, B. (Family Caregiving)
  see N.Y. State Office for the
       Aging
Sommers, T. (Women & Aging)

CENSUS 1980

Siegel, J.S. (1980 Census)

CHILDLESSNESS

Singh, B.K.

CHRONICALLY ILL

Levy, S.M.

CHURCH ATTENDANCE

Alston, Letitia T. (Religion)

CLOTHING

Hoffman, A.M.
Richards, M.L.
Spruiell, P.R.

COMPETENCY AND ABILITY

Giesen, C.B.

CONGRESSIONAL HEARINGS AND REPORTS

U.S. Cong. Congressional Budget
  Off.
U.S. Cong. House. Select Comm.
  on Aging   (Impact)
"   "   (National)
"   "   (Problems)
"   "   (Treatment)
"   "   (Women & Retirement)
"   "   (Women in Midlife)

CONSERVATION ABILITY

Selzer, S.C.

CONSUMERS

Schutz, H.G.
Spruiell, P.R.

COSMETICS

Palmer, M.H.

COUNSELING

Brebner, R.A.
Keller, J.F.
Parham, I.
Wolleat, P.L.

CREATIVITY

Crosson, C.W.
Riley, M.W. (Old)
Willemsen, E.W.

CRIME AGAINST THE AGED

    Humphrey, J.A.
    Lee, G.R.
    U.S. Bureau of the Census
      (Statistical)

CROSS-SECTIONAL STUDIES

    Antonucci, T.C. (Longitudinal)

DAYDREAMS

    Giambra, L.M.

DEATH

    O'Laughlin, K.
    Tate, L.A.

DEPRESSION, FINANCIAL

    Elder, G.H.

DEPRESSION, MENTAL

    Gesino, J.P.

DIRECTORIES

    Cole, K.W.
    Doss, M.M.
    Estes, R.J.
    Everywoman's Guide to Colleges
      and Universities
    Federation of Organizations for
      Prof. Women
    Kruzas, A.T.
    Shields, L.
    U.S. Women's Bureau (Selected)

DISABILITY

    Colvez, A.

DISCRIMINATION IN EMPLOYMENT

    Cameron, C.
    Davidson, J.L. (Issues)
    Leonard, F. (Not Even)
    Matthews, J.L.
    Quinn, J.F.
    Working Women

DISEASES

    Colvez, A.
    Jackson, J.J.
    Kannel, W.B.
    Lake, A.
    Notelovitz, M.
    Porcino, J.
    Sauer, H.I.
    Sommers, T. (Women & Aging)
    Statistical Bulletin
    U.S. Nat'l Ctr. for Health
      Statistics (Health, U.S. 1982)

DISENGAGEMENT THEORY

    Thurmond, G.T.

DISPLACED HOMEMAKERS

    Barrow, G.M.
    Benokraitis, N.
    Cameron, C.
    Leonard, F. (Disillusionment)
    Shields, L.
    Sommers, T. (Epilogue)

DISSERTATIONS

    Mueller, J.E.
    University Microfilms Inter-
      national

DIVORCE

    Benson, H.A.
    Cameron, C.
    Cauhape, E.
    Cherlin, A.
    Chiriboga, D.A.
    DeShane, M.R.
    Johnson, E.S. (Older)
    Leonard, F. (Disillusionment)
    O'Farrell, B.
    Pellegrino, V.Y.
    Rogers, N.
    Uhlenberg, P. (Divorce)

DRUG ABUSE

    Porcino, J.

King, N.R. (Issues)
Lake, A.
LaRue, A.
Markson, E.W.
Nathanson, C.A.
Nat'l Council on the Aging (Fact)
N.Y. (City). Dept. for Aging
Notelovitz, M.
Nudel, A.
Older Women's League Educ.
  Fund (Growing)
Porcino, J.
Sommers, T. (Older Women & Health)
Statistical Bulletin
Taeuber, C.M.
U.S. Bureau of the Census
  (Social & Economic Characteristics)
U.S. Nat'l Ctr. for Health
  Statistics (Health, U.S. 1980)
  "   "   (Health, U.S. 1982)
U.S. Nat'l Inst. on Aging (Special)
Verbrugge, L.M.

HEALTH CARE--UTILIZATION

Hing, E.
Martin, C.A.
U.S. Nat'l Ctr. for Health
  Statistics (Basic)
Verbrugge, L.M.

HEALTH CLUBS

Jacobs, R.H. (Out of)

HISTORY

Fox, V.C.
Gratton, B. (Labor)
Haber, C.
Hendricks, J.
King, N.R. (Issues)
Lopata, H.Z. (Economic)
O'Neill, J.A. (Women)
Rosen, E.
Segalla, R.A.
Seltzer, M.M.
Stratton, J.L.
U.S. Bureau of the Census
  (Social & Economic Status)
Williamson, J.B. (Politics)

HOME CARE

Archbold, P.
Brody, E.M.
Crossman, L.
Fengler, A.P. (Wives)
Shanas, E.
U.S. President's Advisory Comm.
  for Women

HOMEMAKERS

Andre, R.
Burkhauser, R.V. (Challenge)
Cameron, C.
Depner, C.
Gordon, N.M.
Holden, K.C. (Inequitable)
  "   "   (Public)
Meier, E. (New)
O'Farrell, B.
Segalla, R.A.
Szinovacz, M. (Women's
                Retirement)

HOMES FOR THE AGED

Gratton, B. (Labor)
Haber, C.

HOMICIDE VICTIMS

Humphrey, J.A.
Jackson, J.J.

HOMOSEXUALS

Berger, R.M.
Almvig, C.

HOUSEHOLD RESPONSIBLITY

Brubaker, T.H.
Giele, J.Z. (Future Research)
  "   "   (Women's Work)
Keith, P.M. (Sex Differences)
Shanas, E.

HOUSING--RESIDENTS

Carp, F.M.
Fengler, A.P. (Residences)
Lally, M.
Neolker, L.S.
Sullivan, D.A.

LIFE EXPECTANCY

Hendricks, J.
Statistical Bulletin

LIFE INSURANCE

American Council of Life Insurance

LIFE SATISFACTION

Atchley, R.C. (Process)
Beckman, L.J.
Block, M.R. (Professional)
Fengler, A.P. (Residences)
Johnson, E.S. (Suburban)
Keith, P.M.   (Working)
Liang, J.
Riddick, C.C.
Szinovacz, M. (Women's Retirement)
Tate, L.A.
Ward, R.A.

LIFE STYLE

Cauhape, E.
Fuller, M.M.
Hand, J.
Johnson, E.S. (Surburban)
Lally, M.
N.Y. (City). Dept. for Aging
O'Rand, A.M. (Women)
Rosen, E.
Schutz, H.G.
Segalla, R.A.
Sommers, T. (Women & Aging)
Streib, G.F.
Thurmond, G.T.
U.S. Dept. of HEW (Report)
Zube, M.

LIVING ARRANGEMENTS

Block, M.R. (Women)
Crystal, S.
Glick, P.C.
Jackson, J.J.
Johnston, D.F
Masnick, G.
N.Y. (City). Dept. for Aging
Porcino, J.
Streib, G.F.
U.S. Bureau of the Census
   (Social & Economic
    Characteristics)

LONGEVITY

U.S. Nat'l Inst. on Aging (Special)

LONGITUDINAL STUDIES

Antonucci, T.C.
Chirikos, T.N. (Sex)
Hyman, H.H.
Livson, F.B.
Martin, C.A.
O'Rand, A. (Midlife)
Parnes, H.S.

LOSS, PSYCHOLOGICAL

Elder, G.H.

MANAGEMENT

Carr-Ruffino, N.

MARITAL STATUS

Brubaker, T.H.
Chan, T.
Fuller, M.M.
Glick, P.C.
Holden, K.C. (Spouse)
Jackson, J.J.
Longino, C.F.
Markson, E.W.
O'Rand, A. (Midlife)
Porcino, J.
Reno, V.
Sommers, T. (Epilogue)
Taueber, C.M.
Treas, J.   (Marriage)
U.S. Bureau of the Census
   (Social & Economic
    Characteristics)
U.S. Dept. of HEW. (Report)

MARRIAGE

Bradford, L.P.
Williamson, J.B. (Aging)
Willing, J.Z.

MEMORY

Lake, A.
Weinstein, C.E.

MENOPAUSE

Block, M.R. (Women)
Kahana, B.
Kerzner, L.J.
Lake, A.
Norman, W.H.
Notman, M.T.

MENTAL HEALTH

Block, M.R   (Women)
Gelfand, D.E. (Mental)
Gonzalez Del Valle, A.
Grady, S.C.
Kahana, B.
Kivnick, H.Q. (Grandparenthood)
   "   "   (Meaning)
N.Y. (City). Dept. for the Aging
Porcino, J.
Rathbone-McCuan, E. (Pilot)
Taylor, S.P. (Mental)

MENTAL ILLNESS

Vitaliano, P.P.

MIDDLE AGE

Attwood, W.
Brown, E.T.
Giele, J.Z. (Women in the)
Holt, M.E.
Jennings, J.T.
King, N.R. (Issues)
Kubelka, S.
Lake, A.
Livson, F.B.
Norman, W.H.
Pellegrino, V.Y.
O'Rand, A. (Women)
Segalla, R.A.
Shaw, L.B. (Unplanned)
U.S. Cong. House. Select
   Comm. on Aging (National)
   "   "   (Women in Midlife)

MINORITIES

Block, M.R. (Women)
Cole, K.W.
Cuellar, J.B.
Jackson, J.J.
Lesnoff-Caravaglia, G. (Black)
Older Women's League Educ.
   Fund (Growing)

MORALE

Jaslow, P.
Liang, J.
Thurmond, G.T.

MORTALITY

Baker, D.
Fingerhut, L.
Helsing, K.J.
Hendricks, J.
Jackson, J.J.
Kannel, W.B.
Kastenbaum, B.
Nathanson, C.A.
Sauer, H.I.
Shock, N.W. (Biological)
Statistical Bulletin
U.S. Nat'l Ctr. for Health
   Statistics (Advance)
   "   "   (Annual)
   "   "   (Health, U.S. 1980)
   "   "   (Health, U.S. 1982)
Verbrugge, L.M.
Vitaliano, P.P.

MOTHER-DAUGHTER RELATIONSHIP

Cohler, B.J. (Mothers)
Johnson, E.S. (Older)
   "   "   (Role)

NURSING HOMES--RESIDENTS

Helsing, K.J.
Patrick, C.H.
U.S. Bureau of the Census
   (Social & Economic Characteristics)
U.S. Nat'l Ctr. for Health
   Statistics (Health, U.S. 1980)
   "   "   (Health, U.S. 1982)
Vitaliano, P.P.

NUTRITIVE SUPPLEMENTS

Harrill, I. (Dietary)
   "   "   (Relationship)

OBESITY

Hartz, A.J.
Malvestuto, P.

Harris, L.
Henretta, J.C.
Jaslow, P.
Karp, D.A.
Kasworm, C.
Markson, E.W.
Newman, E.S.
O'Rand, A.M.   (Delayed)
Osgood, N.J.
Patrick, C.H.
Paul, C.E.
Szinovacz, M.   (Beyond)
  "   "   (Research)
  "   "   (Service)
  "   "   (Women's Adjustment)
  "   "   (Women's Retirement)
U.S. Nat'l Inst. on Aging (Special)

RETIREMENT, ADJUSTMENT TO

Atchley, R.C.   (Process)
Block, M.R.   (Professional)
Bradford, L.P.
Brubaker, T.H.
Depner, C.
Dienstfrey, H.
Gratton, B.   (Decision)
Jewson, R.H.
Keith, P.M.   (Working)
Levy, S.M.
Nudel, A.
Sommers, T.   (Women & Aging)
Szinovacz, M.   (Personal)
  "   "   (Retirement)
  "   "   (Service)
  "   "   (Women's Adjustment)
  "   "   (Women's Retirement)
Willing, J.Z.

RETIREMENT AGE

Burkhauser, R.V. (Relationship)
Campbell, S.

RETIREMENT GUIDES

Rose, H.

RETIREMENT PLANNING

Behling, J.
Block, M.R. (Professional)
Dissinger, K.
Jewson, R.H.
Kroeger, N.
Olson, S.K.

Szinovacz, M. (Retirement)
  "   "   (Women's Adjustment)
  "   "   (Women's Retirement)

RURAL WOMEN

Braito, R.
Hooyman, N.R.
Mindel, C.H.
Scott, J.P.
Thurmond, G.T.
Wilkinson, C.W.

SELF-APPRAISAL

Kivett, V.R.
LaRue, A.

SELF-ESTEEM

Antonucci, T. (Values)
Puglisi, J.T.
Turner, B.F. (Self)

SELF-PERCEPTION

Rubin, L.B.
Steitz, J.A.
Turner, B.F. (Self)

SENIOR CENTER PROGRAMS

Wilson, M.M.

SEX COMPARISONS/DIFFERENCES

Arens, D.A.
Atchley, R.C. (Process)
Babchuk, N.
Behling, J.H.
Burkhead, D.J.
Chirikos, T.N. (Sex & Race)
Costello, M.T.
Depner, C.
Dillingham, A.E.
Giambra, L.M.
Gibson, R.C. (Race)
  "   "   (Work)
Grad, S.
Gratton, B. (Decision)
Jackson, J.J.
Kahana, B.
Keith, P.M. (Life Changes &)
  "   "   (Life Changes, Leisure)
  "   "   (Sex Differences)

STRESS AND CRISES

SUBURBAN WOMEN

SUICIDE

SUPPLEMENTAL SECURITY INCOME

SUPPORT SYSTEMS

TIME

UNEMPLOYMENT

U.N. CONFERENCE, COPENHAGEN 1980

VOCATIONAL GUIDANCE

   Brebner, R.A.
   Doss, M.M.
   U.S. Women's Bureau (Selected)

VOLUNTEERS AND VOLUNTARISM

   Babchuk, N.
   Nudel, A.

WAGES

   Pursell, D.E.
   Quinn, J.F.
   Shaw, L.B. (Problems)

WELL-BEING

   Keith, P.M. (Life Changes,
               Leisure)
   "   "   (Sex Differences)
   Serow, W.J.

WHITE HOUSE CONFERENCE ON AGING

   Older Women's League Educ.
     Fund (Growing)
   Older Women's League.
     Nat'l Off.
   Sommers, T. (1981 WHCOA)

WIDOWS

   Arens, D.A.
   Barrett, C.J.
   Barrow, G.M.
   Beckman, L.J.
   Cameron, C.
   Fengler, A.P. (Residences)
   Ferraro, K.F.
   Fisher, I.
   Fox, V.C.
   Haber, C.
   Helsing, K.J.
   Hendricks, J.
   Holden, K.C. (Spouse)
   Hyman, H.H.
   Kahana, E.F.
   Karp, D.A.
   Kestenbaum, B.
   Loewinsohn, R.J.
   Lopata, H.Z. (Economic)
   "   "   (Meaning)
   "   "   (Widowed)
   "   "   (Widowhood)
   "   "   (Women as)

   Malatesta, V.J.
   Matthews, S.H.
   Nat'l Retired Teachers Assoc.
   Nudel, A.
   Nye, M.B.
   Parham, I.
   Rogers, G.T.
   Scott, J.P.
   Silverman, P.R.
   Thompson, G.B.
   Treas, J. (Aging)
   U.S. Bureau of the
     Census (American)
   U.S. Cong. Congressional
     Budget Off.
   U.S. Nat'l Inst. on Aging (Special)
   Williamson, J.B. (Aging)

WOMEN IN ADVERTISEMENTS

   Hollenshead, C.

WOMEN IN TELEVISION AND MOVING PICTURES

   Allyn, M.V.
   Gerbner, G.
   Stoddard, K.M.

WORLD ASSEMBLY ON AGING, 1982

   International Conf. of Social
     Gerontology
   Non-Governmental Organizations
   U.S. Dept. of State
   World Assembly on Aging